TO SAY GOODBYE IS TO SAY HELLO . . .

Hello to a new life—to a new, freer, more self-assured you. Hello to new ways of looking at the world and of relating to people. *Your divorce can turn out to be the very best thing that ever happened to you!*

CREATIVE DIVORCE

"Touches all the bases . . . excellent and hard to parallel."
—*Publishers Weekly*

"For anyone who has felt the anguish of divorce, *Creative Divorce* will not only provide solace, but will also open the way to self-renewal."
—Lucy Freeman, author of *Fight Against Fears*

"ABSOLUTELY SPECTACULAR. . . . It has got to be the very best book on the subject to come along—it is touching and human and profoundly hopeful."
—Eda LeShan, author of *The Wonderful Crisis of Middle Age*

ABOUT THE AUTHOR: MEL KRANTZLER received his B.A. degree from Queens College, his M.S. degree in Rehabilitation Counseling from San Francisco State College, and was awarded the James H. Woods Fellowship in Philosophy at Harvard University. Since 1961, he has worked as a career and rehabilitation counselor, and in 1972, he established New Horizons, a counseling service for the divorced.

CREATIVE
DIVORCE

*A New Opportunity
for Personal Growth*

By
MEL KRANTZLER

A SIGNET BOOK

NEW AMERICAN LIBRARY

SIGNET TRADEMARK REG. U.S. PAT. OFF. AND FOREIGN COUNTRIES
REGISTERED TRADEMARK—MARCA REGISTRADA
HECHO EN CHICAGO, U.S.A.

SIGNET, SIGNET CLASSIC, MENTOR, ONYX, PLUME, MERIDIAN AND NAL BOOKS *are published by NAL PENGUIN INC.,*
1633 Broadway, New York, New York 10019

FIRST SIGNET PRINTING, JANUARY, 1975

16   17   18   19   20   21   22   23

PRINTED IN THE UNITED STATES OF AMERICA

Acknowledgments

By its very nature, the making of this book has been an affair of people. The experiences of the members of my divorce adjustment seminars are at its center; my debt to these men and women and their courageous commitment to personal growth is incalculable.

The enthusiastic encouragement of Eve Merriam, Leonard Lewin, Al Hart, Herb Katz, Jim Maas, Ann Diamond, Dr. Joel Fort, and Dr. Martin Acker energized me to write about my personal and professional experiences.

The opportunity to put my concepts about the divorce experience into practice and refine the approach presented in these pages was afforded by Dr. Thomas McCormick, Dr. John Palmer, Dr. Gertrude Hengerer, Chet Villalba, Cal Darrow, Dorothy Satir, Sheba Sweet, and Bernice Rollin.

The superb editorial assistance of Barry Schwenkmeyer is evidenced in every chapter of this book. Working with him has been a pleasure as well as a most productive experience.

Ed La Rocque read this manuscript as friend and critic. I am indebted to him for his many insightful suggestions. And Patricia Biondi Lethbridge gave me the kind of empathy and support without which this book would never have been completed.

M. K.

San Rafael, California
July 16, 1973

Contents

INTRODUCTION

The Emotional
Truth of Divorce

I felt like the walking wounded as I mounted the stairs and opened the door of the second-floor apartment I had rented only that morning. Apartment? More like a furnished room with a hint of a kitchen and bathroom, and walls so paper-thin a sneeze would elicit a "bless you" from the tenant next door. I stared at a chair and a sofa-bed. One guest would be a crowd.

The afternoon heat trapped the used smell of drab furnishings and carried up the noise from the decaying business street below. I could almost taste the nausea welling inside me.

So began my life as a single-again man. Two evenings before, my wife and I faced the fact that continued life together was too much for us both. Hastily packed bags, slammed doors, two nights with a friend, and here I was—looking blankly at the efficiency kitchen on the opposite wall of my new "home." Suddenly the consequences of what I had done rushed in and terrified me. How could I—a career and family counselor, of all people—end up in this predicament? What made me give up on twenty-four years of married life with an attractive, intelligent woman and two delightful teen-age daughters? Why, at the age of fifty, was I leaving behind a large, comfortable home in a quietly genteel section of San Francisco? For this?

Here in this apartment, a few miles and several worlds away from where I had lived, I felt like the loneliest man in the world. My internal inventory was zero. Looking back, I could see only failure and guilt—and ahead, a vortex of emptiness, fear, and uncertainty. After twenty-four years of marriage, the prospect of living alone seemed intolerable. When you break the togetherness habit, is this all that's left?

That was June 25, 1970. Three years later I can still recall the day—not, however, as the end of my world, but as the beginning of an enriching and enlivening voyage of self-discovery that has made me a happier and stronger person than I was before. Although I didn't realize it then, I can now see my divorce as the crisis that jolted me out of self-defeating behavior which for most of my married life had gone unexamined. By getting me out of the ruts of my earlier existence, the divorce forced me to take a good look at myself, analyze where I was and how I had gotten there, and set the stage for what has been the most exciting and rewarding period of my life so far.

Of course, hindsight makes this sound easier than it really was. It took me time to come to grips with my feelings. Even with my training and experience as a professional counselor, I was not prepared for the emotional impact of divorce when it hit me. Mine had been an intellectual understanding. I knew the national facts and figures on divorce. I knew that one out of every three marriages in this country ends in divorce, and that the proportion is increasing. I also knew that more and more marriages are breaking up after fifteen years and longer. What I hadn't known until I experienced it myself was what divorce *felt* like. Until then I couldn't appreciate the paralyzing impact that a feeling of failure combined with sudden "aloneness" can produce. It would be many weeks before this paralysis would wear off, and months before I could think of my divorce as anything less than a tragedy.

At some point during the divorce adjustment seminars I have been leading for the past two years the inevitable question arises, "Is divorce harder on men or women?" In one sense this question is meaningless, since divorce strikes at the emotions, and in their emotions men and women are the same. However, out of these seminars (in which women always outnumber men) I have become aware of an especially cruel kind of squeeze play our society applies to the divorced woman in the 1970s.

The women who attend these seminars, like all other modern American women, know that patterns of life are changing rapidly today. They have been bombarded by the media with the idea that there are endless vistas of happiness and fulfillment awaiting the modern woman who has the courage to escape from her cocoon of domesticity. The women's liberation movement, in my opinion one of the healthiest developments in contemporary America, has tapped a rich vein of discontent over the limitations our culture places upon women of every age. As more and more women break through these limitations and move out to become independent persons of their own making, our society can only be the better for it.

Unfortunately the divorced woman—having broken the domestic ties, and eager to reap the benefits of independent life—must still fight a series of internal and external battles she is often unprepared for. She has been encouraged by what she has read and seen on television to strike out on her own, but has no inkling of the inner turmoil that sudden aloneness after years of marriage can produce. No one has told her that kicking the togetherness habit "cold turkey" brings on the emotional shakes and sweats.

As one woman, divorced after twenty-two years of married life, admitted, "I simply had to leave my marriage. It was intolerable. But now I wonder if I did the right thing. At least I knew who I was then: I was a wife, Mrs. Somebody. Now I'm a zero. I can't even get credit in my own name."

One of the major gratifications to emerge from my experience in divorce adjustment counseling—of which this book is a distillation—is to watch the women in my seminars develop inner resources that had been buried during their marriages, and use them to create happy and fulfilling lives as single people. For many of them, divorce marks the first time they have ever been single. Most of us have never known what it means to think, feel, and act single and can be drowned by the emotional waves aloneness sets in motion. Divorced people are sometimes described as being "single again," but in fact may have never functioned as totally independent adults. This is true as well for men, many of whom proceed from a childhood home, through school and the army ("a man's vacation between his mother and his wife"), to marriage.

By coming to terms with ourselves as single people—by accepting the fact that living alone need not mean living lonely—we are laying the groundwork, if we so choose, for future relationships far more satisfying than the ones we left behind.

POOR ME —
WHOEVER THAT WAS

The first three months were hell. Everything was conspiring against me, and I felt powerless to cope. Just tracking down my apartment was a harrowing experience; I became convinced that all landlords and rental agents were con artists. I hated that apartment. The walls were too thin, the bed was uncomfortable, the young man downstairs was always playing his drums. I felt caught in a vise.

And the housekeeping! How could I have taken for granted those chores which my wife had performed all these years, and which I now had to struggle with unassisted? After work I would find myself roaming up and down supermarket aisles, so self-conscious about being a man on what I had always considered woman's turf that I would inevitably forget what I had come to buy in the first place.

The dirty linen was constantly out of control. I could never manage to get to the laundromat before the last shirt or pair of socks was already in the hamper, and would have to make emergency purchases to tide me through the day. Buttons were always missing from just the sports jacket I wanted to wear, and sewing them back on was a task I simply could not face. My cooking was lousy. I could never get all the ingredients assembled at the proper time and the results were stomach-turning.

Insignificant details? Confessions of a male chauvinist pig? Perhaps, but at the time I saw every domestic chore as an accusation, a personal assault on my male identity. The place was a shambles—I'd sooner buy dishes than wash the ones in the sink. Every time I walked into the apartment, it seemed to punish me for walking out on the comfortable home of my past. How I longed for someone to take care of me!

Disgusted with the new "home" and unbearably lonely (no one ever called me!), I began to eat out every night. Frequently a movie followed dinner—I must have seen every movie released during those first two months and after that, a bar. The bar was a place where I could feel sorry for myself, where a drink could substitute for the warmth of love or friendship, where the friendly bartender nodded sympathetically as long as I kept buying the drinks. Best yet, I could smile at the woman four stools away and sometimes get an inviting smile in return. At last! The chance to prove that I am indeed a man, desired by women, and not a rejected husband. Here, at last, I could find a warm body to fill a few empty hours and maybe restore some sense of my manhood.

However, I soon found this scene drab and unfulfilling. A bar is finally a terribly lonely place full of lonely people. Without friendship and understanding, one-night stands—while momentarily diverting—could not provide me with what I was really looking for. Casual sex became the equivalent of masturbation. Staring up at the shadows on the ceiling in the early morning hours, I would still feel alone.

What was happening to me? Here I was, taking a step I knew I wanted to take—a step into freedom, the freedom to be what I wanted. But where was the swinging bachelor life that was supposed to be mine? I had fallen prey to the myth current among many newly-divorced women. "That bastard," they say. "All he has to do is shower and shave, and go out on the town. He's having a ball while I'm stuck with the kids."

Speaking as just one "bastard," I can say that I did not have a ball. Instead of feeling free to go out on the town and hustle women, I felt *compelled* to do so. I was trying to prove that I was a worthwhile person, not a reject. But one morning I woke up and realized I was getting nowhere. I saw that I was transforming my "freedom" into a flight from freedom—from the new life that was mine for the making, if I could only see it that way.

Economic reality provided another reason for calling a halt to my nocturnal prowlings. Now there were two households to maintain on an income that had just managed to support one in the past. Entertainment and constant eating out were hellishly expensive. That, plus the unwelcome news that my income taxes would be twenty percent higher as a result of my single status, forced me to economize. I began staying at home more, and I took a little more interest in cooking.

GOING BACK —
AND LETTING GO

Another myth I laid to rest during these first months was that by simply moving out I was ending my marital relationship. Now we would each go our separate ways, free to do as we pleased. Bring down the curtain. Finis. Begin a new play, written and directed by me. Right? Wrong. A long-term relationship, particularly when children are involved, doesn't end that way at all. In the months ahead I was to see my wife for many reasons. Sometimes it was to settle legal questions of support for the children, visitation arrangements, or division of household property. Sometimes it was just to pick up a suit, a book, or a piece of furniture I needed. And now I realize that I *manufactured* reasons for going back. I didn't want to ring down the curtain yet.

Of course there were arrangements to be made. I knew that, although we were to become "ex-husband" and "ex-wife," we would never be, nor want to be, "ex-parents." Our children's welfare constituted a valid reason for getting together; and since, for a variety of reasons, my divorce followed the actual separation by more than a year, my wife and I often had to meet to discuss economic and legal problems.

The economic and legal wrangling that poisons many divorces can drag out the emotional letting-go; indeed the very wrangling can become a kind of intense and extremely destructive emotional relationship. That this was not true for me is due in large measure to the cooperation and intelligence of my wife. Both of us had known divorced people who continued their marital battles in the courtroom and used their children as weapons against each other. We were both determined to keep ourselves and our children from becoming casualties in that kind of war.

Looking back I now realize how much my former wife made this possible. It has taken time for me to come to this understanding. Now I can view her as a separate person who is different from me. Three years ago, each of us was a monster in the other's eyes; today we are normal, fallible human beings, struggling in different ways to make better lives for ourselves.

In the beginning, however, I wasn't nearly so clear-sighted. I was totally unprepared for the devastating impact each meeting with my wife had on my emotions. Each meeting stirred up enormously conflicting feelings that left me shaken for days afterward. I remember the first time—three weeks after I moved out—I went to visit my wife to arrange child support and visitation procedures. I thought it would be easy enough; after all, she and I were both civilized people, weren't we? But as my car approached the old neighborhood I felt a surge of nostalgia for the "good old days," and I panicked. *What* good old days? This wasn't what I was supposed to be feeling. I had said good-bye to all that, hadn't I? I had consciously chosen a different way of living. Had I made a mistake?

I drove around that familiar block three times before I mustered the courage to park and walk up the steps to the front door. Getting up those steps took an eternity. On this comfortable suburban street I found that the past three weeks of my life suddenly seemed even more tawdry than they were. The lonely evenings, the one-night stands, all those dirty dishes—maybe we could try it again, maybe we had "learned our lesson," maybe the separation had jolted us enough so that we could discover new joys in our marriage.

Even as part of my mind rejected this hope of pure fantasy, at a deep emotional level I wanted it to come true. And with this longing, irrational as it may appear, came fear and hostility—fear that she would not accept me, hostility at her rejection.

A jangle of confusion, I rang the bell.

What happened? Nothing much, on the surface. No shouting, no screaming, no throwing of pots and pans, certainly no passionate reunion. Curt nods, mumbled hellos, and then down to business to curtain off our so very vulnerable emotions. I found myself looking as if for the first time at a woman I had spent twenty-four years with. As our discussion proceeded, I yearned for some sign—a gesture, an open-ended phrase, a nuance—to feed my fantasy, but saw only the reality that our marriage had ended.

It was a scene we were to repeat many times in the ensuing months. Each meeting would rekindle—and then dash—my fantasies. I can now see that I was going through the normal crisis of the emotional divorce—the painful but necessary act of reconfirming that the relationship is over emotionally as well as legally. And this very process, necessary though it was, reinforced the overpowering sense of loss and abandonment I felt. I could see that returning to the old relationship was impossible, but what did I have to replace it?

MAKING FRIENDS
WITH MYSELF

As a man, I had a resource for renewal and continuity which many women do not: my job. During this time I continued to work every day, more as an act of will than desire. My job was an interesting one, but now it had lost its savor. I was bleeding inside while trying to help my clients patch up their own emotional wounds. I radiated tenseness and discomfort to others in my office, and they began to look at me with wary eyes. Aware of this, I overcame my feelings of shame and told them of my separation. To my surprise, they responded with warmth, understanding, and a certain relief that it wasn't "more serious." I will always remain grateful for their concern and support. They created an atmosphere of acceptance that enabled me to regain my normal working capacity—to maintain my professional identity, at least—far more quickly than I could have done otherwise.

My first step back up the ladder of self-esteem was to get out of that wretched furnished apartment. Even though I lived there three months, I never got used to it. Whenever I was there I felt uptight, restless, fearful of what was happening inside me. It came to symbolize for me the mess I had made of my life.

New, more positive feelings were starting to surface inside me. I was beginning to accept *in my emotions* that living alone was the inescapable fact of my present life, even though I still felt strongly the pull of my past. Instead of feeling sorry for myself most of the time, I began to direct my energies to immediate, real problems. I still felt uncertain and scared, but I was beginning to recognize that I would have to live with these feelings. I was beginning to think single, feel single—and act on these feelings.

So I rented an unfurnished apartment on the southern fringe of the city—larger, quieter, and most important, newly painted and completely devoid of any traces of previous occupancy. It was mine to furnish as I wanted.

My new apartment was the outward manifestation of my internal house-ordering. I was surprised to find the challenge of furnishing and decorating less overwhelming than I had thought. In fact, I liked to rummage through furniture stores or garage sales on a Saturday afternoon, and took great pride in finding the "perfect" chair or bookcase at a bargain price. I spent a lot of time arranging furniture and bric-a-brac, and browsing through print shops.

With the rooms in order, I felt a new need to keep the place clean—never again that furnished garbage dump I had called home for three months. When the dishes were dirty, I washed them. Problems of food and laundry, which I had blown up to unmanageable proportions, no longer defeated me. I diligently scrutinized newspaper ads for the supermarket specials and department store sales. Preparing my own meals became a pleasure, especially when I successfully mastered a new recipe. I bought a needle and thread and started sewing on buttons, instead of complaining helplessly that the fates were against me.

Let me not overstate my passion for housework. I'm afraid I still regard washing dishes, vacuuming, and lugging dirty clothes to the laundry as distasteful chores. And I must confess to moments—generally while pushing a shopping basket around a supermarket—when I felt this really was woman's work. Suffice it to say that male chauvinist piggism dies hard. The point is that I now accepted these tasks for what they were—necessary to comfortable living—and not daily reminders that I was an abandoned husband and a worthless person.

Within a month of moving into my new apartment, I had made friends with it—and was beginning to make friends with myself again. Gone was that driving need of the first few months to run away, out into the night. When five o'clock rolled around at the office, I no longer panicked over how I could possibly fill the evening hours. My apartment was quiet and spacious enough to provide a pleasant atmosphere for reading, listening to music, or just meditating. More important, I began to see myself as an independent person with *choices*. I could go home and enjoy a quiet evening with myself, if I wanted to; or I could go to a movie or a concert; or I could go out with a friend. I could. It was up to me. I was learning to separate out "living alone" from "living lonely."

FRIENDS —
MINE, HERS, OURS?

As I gradually lost the sense of loneliness when I stayed at home, I took a renewed interest in seeing old friends. My earlier efforts had been disastrous, and only confirmed the fear that I had lost something by living alone. Some couples I had known for twenty years neither called me up nor responded to notes I sent them. An old friend I met on the street one day couldn't get away fast enough; he acted as if I had a contagious disease.

With my increasing self-confidence I took the initiative and got on the telephone. My friends' reactions were surprising and, on the whole, gratifying. Most sounded genuinely delighted to hear from me (many of them had no idea where I was) and were truly concerned about what I was doing with my life. One friend told me he hadn't called because he really didn't know how he was supposed to behave. As he said, "Am I supposed to congratulate you or express my condolences?"

There were those who "took sides" and I could quickly tell whose side they took. There were others who seemed uninterested in maintaining contact, a reaction that puzzled me until I realized that for them I had been merely one half of a couple—part of a social unit suitable for bridge games and dinner parties, but of little use without my mate. I soon learned, however, that even for those married friends (and most of my friends were married) who wanted to keep up our relationship, the realities of social life in this country make single people hard to fit into traditional patterns of entertaining and getting together. Also, as a single man, I presented a threat to my married friends as a potential home-wrecker, a reaction which operates much more strongly against divorced women, but which men experience as well.

I learned three important lessons from taking the risk of reaching out to old friends. I found much more warmth and acceptance than I had thought possible. I came to accept the rejections I got not as rejections of me, but as an unwillingness to accept me as a single-again person. I saw that my divorce was itself a profoundly threatening event in the lives of some of my friends. As one man later told me, "We always thought your marriage was one of the perfect ones. If divorce could happen to you, what about the rest of us?"

Finally, it became evident that I would have to supplement my old friends with new friends who fit my pattern of single life. This I began to do, encouraged by the results of my own initiative with friends of long standing. I began to make a conscious effort to introduce myself to men and women at parties or business meetings, to initiate conversations at concerts or lectures with women I found attractive. At an age when most people stop making new friends, I took some pride in my newfound ability to seek out and develop rewarding new personal relationships.

MY CHILDREN
ARE PEOPLE, TOO

From the beginning, I had been most concerned about my daughters. Nothing depressed me as much as the thought of missing out on their development into independent young women. In that lousy furnished apartment I realized for the first time how acutely I missed their daily presence, if only at the dinner table. Even though my wife had been extremely generous in volunteering flexible visitation rights, arranging meetings was always complicated. I took every hassle as a rejection. Why should they always have dates on the Saturday when I wanted to see them?

Until my own internal conflicts subsided, these visits were full of tension. From them, awkward attempts at small talk, barely-veiled distaste at Dad's new "home," and eyes full of hurt and puzzlement. From me, one frantic, gala evening after another—concerts, plays, movies, fancy restaurants. I had fallen into the Disneyland-Daddy trap. What was I trying to do? Make them love me? Give them a taste of what they were missing by not being with me? Show up my wife? Hide the real truth of my barren existence? Fill up the time with frenetic activity so we wouldn't have a chance to talk about what happened? All of these things, probably, and I succeeded no more than other fathers do, which is to say not at all. They say today's kids are "too cool to con." In the realm of emotions this has always been true for all children, who are far more adept than adults at sorting out the emotional truth of a situation from among the lies and rationalizations we feed them.

As I began to understand more about what was happening inside me, I started to take a new look at my relationship with my children. In the final years of my marriage I had been so wrapped up in my own concerns that I had taken them for granted. Like most fathers, I loved them deeply, but I expressed my love in the superficial: How was school today? What grade did you get? Where are you going tonight, and what time will you be home?

Just as divorce was the beginning of a creative period of growth for me, it was the catalyst for a deeper relationship with my daughters. One Saturday when they came to visit me in my new apartment (what a boost it gave me to see their surprise and delight at how their "messy" father had fixed up his new place!), we didn't go anywhere. We just sat and talked. I tried to take my cues from what they wanted—and what they wanted was to know what my life was like. How did I—the man who couldn't boil an egg—manage to cook for myself? What was I doing with myself? We talked about my previously untapped decorator's skill. They made a few sensible furniture rearrangements, and insisted on doing some housecleaning. When dinnertime came, they suggested we prepare it together and not go out to eat. A few days later I received in the mail some handwritten, easy-to-follow recipes from them, which I put to good use.

The flow of that Saturday was delightful, full of small talk, comfortable daily routine, and aglow with a family feeling I sorely needed. Everything my daughters did told me more strongly than words that they wanted to be part of my new life. In that atmosphere, I was encouraged to tell them what I was going through. Haltingly, and with more than a little fear of rejection, I was leveling with my children.

For the first time in my life, I tried stepping out from behind the "father" stereotype to expose myself as a real, fallible, far-from-omnipotent human being. The risk was well taken. Instead of rejection and confusion, I found warmth and empathy and eyes that glistened with love. My daughters, in turn, began to open up with me. To my astonishment, they said they had been aware of the growing conflicts between their parents, and that our divorce, when it finally came, was no surprise to them. And I had thought we had always covered up when the children were around! What we had succeeded in doing instead was to make them feel responsible. They assumed we had stayed together as long as we had just for them. I was happy to be able to relieve their feelings of guilt on that score.

That Saturday marked the beginning of a new era between me and my daughters. We began to look at each other as people, not as actors in a family drama. Our new understanding enabled me to accept the fact that I would be seeing them less frequently than in the past. The rewards of our relationship in the future would come from the quality, and not the quantity, of the time we spent together.

HOLIDAY
SETBACKS

I had been living alone five months when Thanksgiving rolled around and exploded in my face. We had agreed that I would celebrate Thanksgiving on Friday with my daughters (I was learning that day-old holidays could be one of the by-products of divorce) but Thanksgiving day itself really unhinged me. I spent that day alone in my apartment sorrowing for the warmth, bustle, good food, and happy times of the past. I drowned myself in memories that day, and for more than one moment I had a wild urge to call my ex-wife and say, "Let's try it again, we really can make a better life together." Each time, however, reality would raise its ugly head, and I would be thrown back on my grief. The next day's visit with my daughters helped mitigate my pain, but of course it wasn't the same.

Christmas was worse. The children had asked for a family Christmas but I simply couldn't face the thought. Reality was painful enough; to pretend that we were still a family would be excruciating. As on Thanksgiving, I celebrated Christmas one day late with my daughters, As on Thanksgiving, I was alone on Christmas and wept without shame over my own solitary state and for the past I would never know again.

I was to experience other setbacks as time went on, but Christmas was my nadir. Everything I saw reminded me of what I didn't have—families shopping together, parents and children gathered around the Christmas tree, couples on their way to parties. During that season, I saw the whole world in "twos" and I felt very much like a severed half.

Eventually, I began to climb out of my hole of self-pity and self-hatred—two steps forward, one step back. The tremendous surge of nostalgia that almost drowned me during those first holidays now subsided. What helped me most was the dawning awareness that my grief was natural and inevitable. I was mourning the death of a twenty-four-year relationship which, in spite of all its agony, held many, many happy memories for me. My grief was normal, and only time could assuage it.

WOMEN: COME CLOSE, BUT GO AWAY

By about the seventh month, I had recovered enough of my self-esteem to take a good look at who I really was. By then I realized that I was not the only person in the world ever to suffer through a divorce. I discovered that behind the statistics that produce articles like "Soaring Divorce Rates: Our National Disgrace," was a world of "nice" people—single-again men and women in the same stages of emotional disarray I was going through. I collared friends, acquaintances, even total strangers—anyone with a personal story of divorce to tell. And what a relief it was to share my feelings. Until then, I had thought my reactions were unique. Nobody could have felt my kind of pain, my kind of self-doubt!

Now time had healed my emotional wounds sufficiently so that I could apply my professional training and experience as a counselor to my own situation. By now, I had gained enough perspective on those first months to recognize them as a necessary period of mourning for a dead relationship that all divorced people must go through. I was ready to take a look at how I was handling my new life.

The subject of women forced me into some serious introspection. By this time I had outgrown the bar scene. I wanted a more satisfying long-term relationship full of friendliness, warmth, and sharing, with a woman who would accept me for what I was rather than for what I should be.

I started dating again (although applying that outmoded word to the social activities of a middle-aged man never ceased to make me feel foolish). During these months I went out with several women whom I found attractive, interesting, and fun to be with, and who seemed to enjoy my company. Somehow, though, these relationships never amounted to anything. At a point, "something" would happen, we would part, and I would be left with a feeling of emptiness.

The clincher came when a woman I had been hotly pursuing for three weeks told me, politely enough, to get lost. I had thought we were getting along splendidly. She was it, the new love of my life! After our first date I had gone home and spun out a complete fantasy which took us through an enchanting courtship and a marvelous marriage. Her turn-off sent me into a nosedive. This time however, instead of grabbing my little black book and reaching for the telephone, I took the advice I was always giving my clients: *get in touch with your feelings*. I spent the next few evenings alone at home with the lights turned low, and waited in the quietness around and within me for my feelings to well up to the level of my consciousness. I let them visit with me because they were mine—ugly, yes, and distortive of external truth, but real and true reactions of a person in pain. I felt rejected. That bitch! How dare she! I felt abandoned and victimized and *hostile:* if she didn't love me, she was a monster! Who was going to give me home-cooked dinners now?

I let these feelings play themselves out by not denying their existence. I went over and over a half dozen recent relationships that had just fizzled out. Gradually a pattern began to emerge.

Here is what I learned: each relationship started out on a high social level—dinners out, concerts, good conversation—and then moved to a more relaxed, domestic scene—home-cooked meals, quiet evenings by the fire, even pleasant sex. Then that "something" happened, and now I could see what it was. As soon as I began to feel close, to experience emotions of affection and tenderness (the very emotions I most desired), a little voice inside me said, "Watch it. This is the kind of closeness that made you marry in the first place, and look what happened. You'd better scram before you get hurt again. Escape while you can."

There it was. Closeness in my mind equaled being hurt. I had created for myself a built-in distancer that guaranteed a future of nothing but unsatisfactory, short-lived affairs. Even though part of me wanted that closeness, a stronger part of me was yelling, "Run, run, run!"

Once I had recognized the pull of the past in operation, my professional training came into play. I knew that the present is not the past. I knew that by increasing my self-awareness I could still that strident voice inside me by telling it, "Today is not yesterday. Today is today. I can break the pattern." This process was not easy, nor did it guarantee automatic success in my future relationships. Intellectual understanding of emotional reality does not produce instant results. But it is the way to begin.

THE MALE CHAUVINIST PIG FACTOR

As my murky conceptions of what I was doing began to clear, a few other unpleasant facts about me came to light. Okay, so I wanted a mature relationship with a warm-hearted, understanding, attractive woman who would love me for what I am. *But what kind of signals was I sending out to attract that kind of woman in the first place?* As I thought about my relations with my ex-wife and with other women in the past months, "hardly any" was the only truthful answer I could give.

I was forced to acknowledge that what I *said* I wanted in a relationship and what I *really* wanted were two different things:

- I said I wanted a woman who was interesting as a person, yet I still viewed women as sex objects and second-class citizens. They were there primarily to listen to my problems and to take to bed.
- I said I wanted a woman to view me with no illusory expectations, but what I really wanted was a woman who would buy my own illusions about myself.
- I said I wanted an open relationship of shared feelings, but I continued to assume I knew what a woman was thinking or feeling without bothering to ask her. She had to live up to my own set of fantasies; never mind what she was really like.
- I said I was ready for a mature relationship between two adults, but what I really wanted was someone to take care of me. I was confusing a home-cooked meal with love.

I could accept accusations of sexism in daily life, but the realization that I was a male chauvinist pig at the emotional level was hard to swallow. I squirmed under the pitilessly bright light of sudden self-knowledge as scenes from the last three weeks replayed themselves in my mind: the impossible demands I made on that woman's time; the incessant talk about *myself* with no thought that *she* might have something to say; all those evenings I had sat in her living room with my drink and the newspaper while she prepared dinner. Had I ever told her how I really felt, or asked her what she was feeling? No wonder she told me to get lost!

Some anthropologists now believe that American men need marriage more than women do. On the other hand, women face pressures in our society which men are free of. Few men have to cope with the problems of the divorced mother trying to juggle her maternal responsibilities with her need to work and establish a new social life. The divorced man may never experience the same degree of fear and uncertainty as the middle-aged divorced woman with grown-up children who is suddenly thrown back into a world which places such a high premium on youth and good looks.

These are real differences. But divorce causes the same feelings of failure, rejection, abandonment, remorse, insecurity, and fear in both sexes. Surprisingly, it matters little in the long run whether the divorce was a mutual decision, or if one partner walked out on the other. In almost all cases, the pain of emotional disentanglement affects each spouse equally, although each may feel the pain in different ways.

As a man living in this society, I had to break through a lifetime of cultural brainwashing in order to discover my feelings. Like all other American males, I held it unmanly to admit to any feelings that undermined the strong-man image society demanded of me. When Susie falls down and skins her knee she can run to Mommy, but Jimmy quickly learns he'd better hide his tears if he wants to avoid being called a sissy. After years of such conditioning, feelings hidden become feelings denied.

When I stopped denying my real feelings, I began to understand how they were frustrating my efforts to get close to women. With this knowledge, I was able to act on my deeply held conviction that the "you are there only for my convenience" behavior (which I now could see was a pattern in my marriage) would get me nowhere in my new life. I became alert to the conflicting signals I was unconsciously transmitting to women ("Love me, but don't get too close"), and as a result began—without pressing—to attract the kind of woman with whom I could establish a close relationship.

There was pain aplenty in this process. I felt tremendous remorse over my marriage. If only I had known this earlier, how different it might have been! Despite my intellectual understanding, ingrained patterns of behavior were hard to break. Even though I could now see in my new relationships that my feelings of hurt and rejection sprang from memories of what past closeness had brought, the pull of the past remained strong.

Nevertheless, the enhanced quality of my life today tells me I am moving in the right direction. By setting aside the motto of "nothing ventured, nothing lost," I have opened myself up to rewarding experiences that were well worth the risk of getting hurt. (As a serendipitous by-product, I now find my circle of friends has expanded to include more women—not as potential bed-partners or dinner-makers, but as interesting and intelligent new people who incidentally are women.)

A NEW OPPORTUNITY FOR PERSONAL GROWTH

Today I look back on the last three years as the most personally enriching period in my life. Through a painful emotional crisis, I have become a happier and stronger person than I was before. I learned that what I went through was what all divorced people, men and women, go through to a greater or lesser degree—first a recognition that a relationship has died, then a period of mourning, and finally a slow, painful emotional readjustment to the facts of single life. I experienced the pitfalls along the way—the wallowing in self-pity, the refusal to let go of the old relationship, the repetition of old ways in relating to new people, the confusion of past emotions with present reality—and I emerged the better for it.

As a professional counselor and a divorced man, I saw divorce as an emotional process with its own internal time schedule that a divorce decree can hasten or delay, but not eradicate. It is a crisis that must be lived through. More than that, however, more than just a time for picking up the pieces, divorce is a new opportunity to *improve* on the past and create a fuller life—*if* you can come to terms with the past, recognize self-defeating behavior, and be willing to change it.

From my professional background as well as my personal experience, I knew that without some kind of outside support these "ifs" would overwhelm almost anyone, let alone men and women caught up in an emotional uproar. Until my own divorce, I had naively assumed that the "helping professions"—social agencies, private community groups—offered services designed specifically for the divorced or separated. Only after I faced the problem myself did I check out this assumption—and found that I was wrong. In spite of its high rate of divorce, the San Francisco Bay area offered no readily-available, inexpensive programs to help divorced people understand what they were going through. Society provides widow's weeds and black armbands for those who have lost a spouse through death, but has nothing to say to the increasing numbers of men and women who need help in getting through the emotional crisis of divorce.

This discovery led to an important change in my working life. I knew from my own experience that divorce, however painful, can signal the beginning of a creative period of self-awareness and growth for people of any age. I saw the need to share this knowledge with other divorced or separated persons who felt trapped and hopeless. I wanted to help them find the means within themselves to make divorce the beginning of a better life, as I did, and not the end.

So in the spring of 1972 I left my job as a family and career counselor with a California state agency, and began a new career as a full-time counselor in divorce adjustment problems. As several colleagues who tried to dissuade me pointed out, self-employment is a risky business, especially in a new field. Nevertheless, the response so far has more than justified whatever risk I took, and the growing national interest in the problems of the divorced person convinces me I made the right decision.

Drawing on my professional background and personal experience, I now lead counseling groups, workshops and college seminars to help people cope with the trauma of divorce. By talking together, participants experience the "I am not alone" feeling that was so essential to the recovery of my own self-esteem. Quickly each member of the group comes to see that, while his or her experience is in many ways unique, there are nevertheless common threads uniting us all. Once these are understood, the process of coming to terms with past marital relationships can begin—and with it the reshaping of inner life and external circumstances into a more satisfying whole. This can happen for anyone who has the desire to change—business and professional men and women, housewives, laborers. In the cauldron of our emotions, we are all the same.

This book is a product of these shared insights. It is written in the hope that you who read it will find pathways to new beginnings, clues to renewing your life and your self out of the traumatic experience of divorce.

CHAPTER 1

The Promise in the Pain

The first step toward making divorce a creative process is to understand what it is—and what it isn't. Divorce is not the judgment of a wrathful society, although the guilt feelings divorce can evoke often makes it seem so. It is not just a termination of legal and economic ties, unless the marriage itself was nothing more than a convenient business or social relationship. Nor is it a kind of real-life parlor game, a battle of intellects in which the partner who remains cool-headed defeats his or her opponent.

Divorce is an emotional crisis triggered by a sudden and unexpected loss. The death of a relationship is the first stage in a process in which the death is recognized, and the relationship is mourned and then laid to rest to make way for self-renewal. Intellectually, a newly separated person may deny being in crisis, but it is there to see in everything he or she does. Suddenly normal ways of coping do not seem to work. Overnight the world has changed into a frightening question mark, and everyday life is out of control. Simple decisions are no longer manageable; even getting dressed in the morning is difficult and often not worth the effort.

As human beings we cannot tolerate this "sink or swim" state of affairs for very long. After the initial shock, each of us begins the painful process of restoring balance to our lives. We develop new ways of coping with the crisis in a frantic effort to reduce the internal tensions it has produced. In the process we invariably tap resources and abilities we never knew we had, although in the first stages of our separation we may be in too much pain to recognize them.

THE DIVORCE CRISIS:
HELEN'S STORY

I first met Helen at the opening session of one of my earliest divorce adjustment seminars. Dressed in a well-cut, beige pantsuit that set off her auburn hair, she walked into the room as if she were walking out, headed for a chair in the farthest corner, and proceeded to try to make herself invisible. Her only activity was a frequent search for a handkerchief when her tears began to spill. Behind the red eyes and tight lips I thought I detected an attractive woman, but on this evening emotional disarray was blotting out the person behind the pain.

At that first session we learned only that she was Helen Randall, 36, the mother of two children aged eight and twelve, and separated nine weeks after a fourteen-year marriage. Her story, which was to unfold in the weeks that followed, exemplifies a common pattern of marriage and divorce, and highlights the dynamics of the divorce crisis which can make it a launching pad for personal growth.

Their split-up was violent and, as Helen remembers it, totally unexpected. It happened the day she came home late from an afternoon noncredit course in art history she was taking at a local college and found Bob struggling with dinner in a smoke-filled kitchen and two sullen children sitting in the living room.

"No one got dinner that night," Helen remembers. "Before I could tell him why I was late, he started accusing me of neglecting him and the kids, and making nasty cracks about what the professor and I had been doing after class broke up. I remember saying something like, 'It takes one to know one.' Then we really started screaming at each other, and he went for his suitcase and I started throwing his clothes on the bed. When he was getting into the car I actually stood on the front steps and threw a pair of shoes at him."

That night Helen slept on the couch and, although she later moved into the guest room, she still has not been able to bring herself to sleep in the master bedroom. "I was sure at first he would come back, that he would miss the kids and me so much he would admit his mistake and come home. But he didn't."

In those first weeks Helen said she felt almost dead. "I don't really know what I felt. Half the time I was furious. The first time I had to figure out how to start the lawn mower I had an overwhelming wish that he was lying in front of it. I really think I could have pushed it right over him. But then in the evenings I would get so lonely that I wished he were there. One night I woke up about three o'clock and thought I heard a funny noise outside. I automatically reached for Bob and when I realized he wasn't there I got terrified. If it hadn't been so late, I think I would have called him up. I eventually got back to sleep, but I kept having nightmares about the time when I was a little girl and got lost in the woods behind our house."

Nine weeks after her separation, Helen had still not told her parents. "I don't think they could take it. There's never been a divorce in our family before, except for an aunt of my mother's who we never saw and almost never talked about. My mother is very much the dedicated housewife and she brought me up to be the same. My father was away a lot when I was growing up, but my mother kept busy with raising her kids and keeping the house looking nice. Whenever he was home, there was no question of who came first in the household. That's what I was always told marriage was like, and I guess I bought the idea. How can I tell them now what a mess their little girl has made of her life?"

In the last two weeks Helen has been getting some pressure from her friend Betty to get out in the world, although she says she doesn't feel up to it yet. "I have been looking at the help-wanted ads, though, and Betty helped me type up a resumé. She included all my volunteer activities and I must admit I was impressed with my list of qualifications. Betty thinks I could get a job at the social-work agency she works for, but I just don't see myself as a professional woman."

Life at home is no longer the frightening hell it was at first, but the house still seems empty and Helen can't work up much interest in housework. "It's as if I threw out one half of myself when I threw Bob out. The kids have tried to understand—Bobby even told me it was nice to have dinner without arguing all the time—but I know it's hard for them. If he hasn't come back by now, I suppose he never will—but when I look around at all my happily married friends, I don't see why this had to happen to me."

Helen arrived at that first session far too upset to view her experience clearly, but in the following weeks she—and the other members of the seminar—came to understand the nature of the crisis they were all experiencing. Subsequent chapters of this book will examine the process of growth the divorce crisis can set in motion. Seizing this opportunity requires an understanding of the crisis itself.

1. *Separation or divorce introduces many new circumstances into our lives which force us out of our daily routines and require new kinds of behavior.* Biologically, we are what we eat. Psychologically, we are what we do. With separation, some of the familiar roles that have defined our lives in the past disappear, and other new roles are thrust upon us. The initial reaction to this sudden change is confusion, fear, and uncertainty. This is normal; our identities are shaped by the roles we play—husband,

wife, lover, parent, breadwinner, homemaker. We derive a great deal of unconscious comfort and security in the familiar routine that goes with being a family man or housewife, even when our marriages turn sour and we find aspects of these roles constricting.

In a world of new situations with none of the familiar guideposts of our married lives each of us has no choice but to begin to behave as a separate person, not one half of a couple. A sudden change in accustomed roles shakes the bedrock of our identity. "Who am I if not a wife/husband?" is the unspoken cry of all divorced or separated people.

The transition to the single role is painful. The promise lies in the fact that new roles force us to tap resources and abilities we never knew we had. Helen finally did figure out how to start the lawn mower, when she had to, and she got the grass cut. A small victory, perhaps, but an important accomplishment for someone who hadn't thought she could do it—and an encouraging step in the process of reviving the separate identity Helen had buried in her role as dependent wife and mother.

2. *The crisis of divorce brings to the surface unresolved feelings from the past that have stood in the way of happiness.* All of us carry around a great deal of excess emotional baggage accumulated during lifetimes of pleasure and pain—not the pleasant mental scrapbooks we leaf through during moments of reverie, but feelings. In divorce, we link the pain we feel with earlier experiences of loss and abandonment. The circumstances may be entirely different, but the feelings are the same. Helen, as a grown-up woman living in a well-protected neighborhood presumably has no rational reason to fear sounds in the night; but at the moment she woke up she was not a grown-up woman in her emotions. She was a child. The 'loss' of her husband (even though *she* kicked *him* out) had triggered feelings of abandonment stemming from her childhood.

The fact that these feelings are so close to the surface during an emotional crisis such as divorce helps us to recognize their power. Awareness of their existence can help explain why we feel emotions—abandonment, hostility, rage, and fear—totally out of proportion to the event that may trigger them. With acceptance can come the understanding that "Yes, I have these feelings from the past and they are real feelings, but they need not define the way I act now. I am not a little girl (or boy) any more."

This process, too, is painful and far from simple, but it offers the opportunity for us to accept our feelings for what they are and thereby blunt their hidden control over our lives. If we continue to deny them, they will not go away. Instead they will remain as a kind of unconscious emotional road map—full of twisting roads, detours, and blind alleys—that prevents us from ever arriving at our destination. The crisis of divorce brings with it the chance to shed light on this road map, straighten out some roads, and avoid blind alleys in the future.

3. *The crisis of divorce releases emotional energies.* In the initial stages of the divorce crisis, when we want at all costs to restore balance to our lives, we become flooded with emotional adrenalin. Consciously or unconsciously, we choose the direction this energy propels us. Like a mother who "miraculously" finds the strength to lift the car from her child trapped beneath it, we can mobilize this energy to move into our fears and uncertainties.

At this stage of Helen's story, she has not yet set her life back on its tracks, but she has taken a first step in getting her resumé together. Instead of channeling her energies into fits of weeping and hysteria, she has used them to constructive purposes. Other divorced or separated people discover the strength to do things they never would have thought themselves capable of—drive a car alone on the highway at night, for example, or make sense out of the family finances. These achievements may be performed more out of desperation than pride, but they are nevertheless signs of abilities and resources that will stand us in good stead as independent people.

WHERE IS SOCIETY'S SUPPORT?

Divorce is by no means the only crisis of loss. Other losses can produce the same kind of emotional turmoil: a woman discovers a tumor on her left breast, a middle-aged man loses his job, a hurricane levels a town on the Texas coast, a young husband is reported missing in action, a child dies. Like divorce, these are all crises of loss which trigger a similar kind of disruption of identity, up-surges of feelings from the past, and heightened emotional energies. In every case those whose lives are touched by crisis immediately begin to restore balance to their lives.

This is not to say, however, that methods of restoring balance are necessarily rational. The woman who finds a tumor on her breast may convince herself that nothing is wrong and never go to her doctor. The man out of work may hole up for months with a bottle of Scotch. A mother whose child dies may not once give in to grief, and never realize the emotional price she has paid for her composure. Denial of loss is human; at first it gives us time to gather strength and establish perspective on a fact of life too threatening to face immediately. Only when we become stuck at this point—in the bottle, in a fantasy world, behind an icy-hard facade—are we in trouble. We may have restored internal balance, but only by obliterating the potential for personal growth the crisis evokes within us.

Society recognizes some kinds of losses. Blankets, food, and messages of support pour in to the town destroyed by a hurricane. The wife whose husband was lost receives personal visits from military representatives. The mother whose child dies attends a funeral. A funeral is society's formal recognition of loss. Although funeral practices vary among cultures, the message is the same. Society is saying, in effect, "Your grief is recognized. It's quite proper to feel as you do. Everyone feels this way when a loved one dies. Here is the way you should express your emotions. You will feel better for it."

Unfortunately, society holds out no such helping hand to divorced men and women experiencing the loss that comes with the death of a relationship. Despite the fact that almost one out of two marriages in this country will eventually break up, our society clings to the belief that nice people don't get divorced. Divorce is accepted among the exotics of our society—film stars, TV performers, and the jet-setters—but it is not for "real people." Just beneath a surface sophistication about new life-styles and the liberated woman persists an attitude best expressed in two paragraphs from something a tearful young woman brought to one of my divorce adjustment seminars:

Failure is not a popular American word, yet every divorce statistic means two people have failed in life's most noble and important relationship—failed themselves, failed their children, failed their Creator, and failed society.

Because our experience proves that most unhappy marriages are merely sick and can be made healthy and happy again, we don't want your marriage to be just another failure.

This is not a nineteenth-century moral tract. It is part of a pamphlet prepared and currently distributed to couples contemplating divorce by the Conciliation Court of Sonoma County's Superior Court, State of California! When the cocktail conversation dies down and the latest magazine articles are set aside, this remains the official judgment society lays on the divorced man or woman: you are a failure. California is by no means a backward state; the fact that in spite of its extremely high divorce rate it can still endorse such sentiments only indicates how deep-seated they are, and how slowly society's moral code changes to encompass new patterns of living.

YOU ARE
NOT ALONE

Given such strong cultural conditioning, I have the greatest respect for the men and women who get up the courage to come to my divorce adjustment seminars and expose themselves as "failures" in the eyes of society. Every opening session is the same: thirty frightened and depressed people poised for flight on the edge of their chairs. Tense, embarrassed, afraid to meet the eyes of the others in the room, they seem surprised to find other people there. Each one had thought he or she would be the only person to show up!

In the next three hours they begin to relax and share experiences. Most of them have never before been in a situation in which they can express their real feelings without fear of being judged. As personal stories haltingly unfold, eyes shift from the cracks in the floor and heads begin to rise. Slowly the atmosphere of a courtroom full of self-admitted criminals awaiting sentence begins to dissipate. Their downcast expressions lift. Here are no jurors sitting in judgment on criminals against society. These are people like themselves going through a common painful experience—young and old, men and women, some married for a short time, others going through a break-up after twenty-five years of married life.

These men and women are typical of the sixteen million Americans who have at one time or another been through a divorce—not freaks or misfits, but normal average people who, with one or two exceptions, are experiencing the dissolution of the only marriage they have ever known. Some are cast-off husbands and wives, abandoned points on the eternal triangle. More, however, are men and women who ended marriages in which they could no longer find the mixture of support and freedom for personal growth.

The number of divorces grows with every decade. Ten years ago 400,000 American couples were divorced; now the number is over 750,000. Statistics tell only part of the story: that one out of every nine adult Americans has been through a divorce; that the typical divorce really does occur during the itchy seventh year, but that more and more marriages of long duration are ending; that this year some 200,000 couples will break up togetherness habits of fifteen years and longer. What statistics do not report are the equal numbers of people who simply walk away from their marriages without bothering to dissolve them legally—and the many divorces which people hide from the census-takers out of a sense of shame and failure. There is cold comfort in statistics to be sure, but they do offer the reassurance that comes from knowing that we are not alone.

FROM THE
FRYING PAN ...

The frightened men and women who attend my seminars come because, like most divorced people, their separation has thrown them into an unfamiliar and threatening world that they are totally unprepared for. Suddenly they are alone, with no one to praise or blame, no one to be insecure with, no one to share with or hide from—except themselves. They are half-persons in a pressure cooker of confusion and misery, desperately seeking an answer for the cry within them, "Dear God, what is happening and why is it happening to me?"

Considering society's attitude, it is not surprising that many have come only as a last resort:

- Marge, 32, abandoned by her husband, has spent the past three months crying constantly. Her two children are out of control. Although she has the money, bills have gone unpaid, and now she has been served an eviction notice.
- Arthur, 44, left his wife to move in with his mistress. Suddenly he finds himself impotent.
- Betty, 40, kicked her husband out of the house when she found out about his long-term affair with his secretary. Now she menstruates every eleven days, leaves the house only for trips to the liquor store, and hasn't answered her phone in four months. Three nights ago the fire department had to rescue her from a blaze started by a cigarette she was smoking when she passed out on the couch.
- Esther, 56, children's editor of a publishing company, came to a mutual parting of the ways with her husband. She thought theirs was a civilized divorce until the day they met in the lawyer's office to discuss division of property—and proceeded to scream at each other for two solid hours. She was so emotionally drained that she couldn't go to work for three days afterward.

The motivation of others is less dramatic but just as compelling:

- George, 38 and father of three, agreed with his wife to call it quits after one knock-down, drag-out battle too many. Now, one year later, he is still in a slump: he misses the children, even the arguments with his wife, and can't get used to waking up in an empty apartment. He never seems to meet any interesting women.
- Carol, 27, dropped out of college to put her husband Bill through law school. Last fall, over his

violent objections, she took an evening course in art education and as a result decided to return to college full time and become an art teacher. When Bill gave her the ultimatum "your home or your career," she chose her career. They have been separated six months, but somehow she can't bring herself to register for any courses.

- Eleanor, 39, put up with her husband's affairs for years, but one day she had had enough and threw him out. She *says* she wants a divorce, but postpones filing the papers in the hope that he will admit the error of his ways and come home. He has been gone three months and she is still waiting—and despairing.

- Frank, 28, cheated on his wife practically from their honeymoon. Last year he finally divorced her and moved in with his latest girl friend. Now he finds himself cheating on her, and is beginning to wonder if he is doomed to repeat the pattern of his marriage even though he isn't married any more.

- Emily, 46, left her alcoholic husband fifteen months ago. Since then she has been able to return to her career as a high-school guidance counselor, is active in local politics, and does a fair amount of socializing, mostly with people from school. She has found, however, that she needs sleeping pills in the evening and that without a mood elevator in the morning—sometimes two—life seems pretty flat.

Problems like these are common to most divorced or separated persons, and yet the vast majority do not seek outside help. Undoubtedly, some are people who really can shed their marriages easily, who can honestly say that getting divorced was like taking off a tight pair of shoes—although the number of such painless partings is far lower than most people think, and possible only when the marriage itself was characterized by an unusual amount of personal and emotional independence for both husband and wife. There are others—the lucky few—who can work through a divorce on their own and eventually arrive at a satisfactory new life free of past limitations and internal stresses.

In my experience, however, they are the exception which proves the rule. Most divorced people in need of help do not seek it because, consciously or not, they have bought society's picture of them as failures. Paralyzed by feelings of guilt and inadequacy, they cling to their private misery-go-round without ever daring to hope that something better is possible They feel they *deserve* whatever suffering they are going through.

No matter how sophisticated society may become, divorce will always be traumatic. As long as we continue to form strong emotional and sexual ties with other people, parting will be painful—whether or not the union was ever recognized in civil or religious ceremony. Divorce can only become a vehicle for creating a better life when we stop thinking of it as *punishment* and start to see it as a *process*—a process over time which begins with the death of a relationship, proceeds through a period of mourning in which the death is recognized and accepted in our emotions, and ends with the rebirth of an independent single person.

CULTIVATE THE SEEDS
BENEATH THE SNOW

Each of us has come to our own separation with a hope that we will find a better life now that our spouse is no longer present. And yet the immediate realities of separation seem to contradict such expectations, especially when they include large components of "instant success" and "overnight change." Many people charge off in search of the big breakthrough, and give up when they don't find it immediately. In so doing they are not only reinforcing their feelings of failure, they are also overlooking some very real signs of personal growth in their daily lives. Some of these signs are to be found in small accomplishments which might seem too trivial to deserve notice; others may appear as nothing more than unpleasant daily reminders of the life that was left behind. Nevertheless, it is precisely because our daily lives tell us in large part who and what we are that even the smallest moves toward living singly merit our recognition and appreciation.

When we feel depressed and negative about ourselves, it is easy to overlook, minimize, or misinterpret these signs. We fear the new; part of us doesn't want to be single, so we cling desperately to the old identity we forged in the furnace of togetherness. We manufacture all kinds of reasons to deny or trivialize the meaning of changes in behavior and feeling brought on by living singly. But these are the first signs of personal growth—the "seeds beneath the snow"—and if we recognize and nurture them, they will eventually yield secure new identities, independent of our former spouses. Here are some of these "seeds" that members of my seminars have shared with each other:

Eating alone with your children. Many parents are so overwhelmed by the empty chair at the table that they ignore the fact that the dinnertime atmosphere may be a lot more pleasant now than it was during their marriage. Ask your children. While you may be preoccupied with feelings of loss and guilt over how your divorce will affect their development in the long run, they may well be relieved at not having to face the screaming arguments and constant bickering that accompanied appetizer, main course, and dessert. (Even if the hostility never erupted in open battle, chances are your children picked up the underlying tension and suffered because of it.) Now is your opportunity to behave toward them as a separate person without fear of censure or angry outbursts from your former spouse.

Mastering the intricacies of the family finances (or a new recipe). In my seminars, reports from men that they cooked and served a complete dinner to their children invariably elicit groans from the women present. In much the same way feminine successes with plumbing repair or income taxes fail to impress the men. "Big deal," is the general reaction, "I've been doing that all my life." Even those who report on mastering a new task often put down their accomplishment. As one man told the group, "I'd hate to think my identity was defined by the ability to stock an empty refrigerator." By the same token, many women fear that doing something "masculine"—having final say on questions of discipline, for example, or dealing assertively with the air-conditioning repairman—puts them in danger of losing their femininity.

These reactions miss the point. In fact, they can destroy the potential for further personal growth such accomplishments represent. If having to stock the refrigerator or do the income taxes is seen as unsexing or inconsequential, then they will be just exactly that. It is only when we realize what such new abilities signify that we can take pride in them. A newly separated woman may curse her absent husband when she has to change a washer, and feel abandoned because she has no one to take care of her. For a man, an empty refrigerator may seem a sign of emotional deprivation. But changing the washer and stocking the refrigerator are tangible signs of personal growth in that both are acts of self-assertion: I can be successful on my own; I can take care of myself. Once understood in this light, these accomplishments become important building blocks in the construction of an independent identity.

Enjoying free time. In the first painful weeks of separation, free time is the last thing most people want. I can still recall my dread of the empty evening hours during the first weeks of my separation. Yet, comforting as a daily routine may appear in retrospect, consider the price one has paid for that security. The most desolate man and woman can usually point to at least one example of welcome free time, even in the initial stages of divorce. As an older woman whose husband had left her confessed, "We always had to have dinner at 6:15 on the dot. The house had to be spotless; if he found dust on the window sill, he would write "dirty" in it. I still miss him, but I must admit it's a relief not to have to dust all day. And now I can eat when *I* feel like it."

One man whose wife had insisted he spend every evening and weekend hour on household improvements and yard work found that, while the pain of initial separation was severe, it was somewhat alleviated by not having to don old clothes after a day at the office and edge the front walk. "I never really liked doing that stuff," he said. "Now I find out I'm really an apartment-dweller at heart. I have no qualms about leaving the joys of fixing the faucet to the superintendent while I relax with a good book."

Every divorced man and woman, if pressed, can think of instances in which newfound free time has led to discoveries about the person they had hidden behind their roles of husband and wife. The mother whose children visit their father on weekends may feel anxious and empty until they return, but during those hours she is practicing a new role as "independent woman" which daily maternal duties had shoved into the background. Probably she won't feel like going out on the town or jetting down to the Caribbean. But she may well visit an old friend, read a book, or just savor the rare freedom of eating when and what *she* wants, watching *her* favorite television program, or sleeping late. Each department from her established routine, however small, is proof of her ability to face—and even enjoy—the facts of single life.

Positive new feelings. These are the easiest signs of personal growth to overlook, since in the initial stages of separation nobody feels very good, but I hear them expressed in my seminars even by those separated for only a few weeks. Women will admit with surprise, "I really thought I would die when he left, but I didn't. I survived!" They report this feeling as a revelation, and revelation it is, for it tells them they are not helpless as they had thought.

Others experience feelings of relief from anxieties and hostilities that had absorbed all their attention toward the end of their marriages. "I don't feel bitchy all the time the way I did when he was home every night," a woman will say. Or, "It's a relief to know that the worst has happened. It's as if the other shoe has finally fallen, and now I can make plans. I still feel miserable, but I'm not nearly as confused and afraid as I was before."

Many working women find increased satisfaction in jobs they had previously considered only in terms of the money they added to their husband's income. One woman whose husband would never admit that her salary from substitute teaching contributed to anything more than clothes for her and their daughter said, "I like my job. I'm a darn good teacher and I know it." More than a statement about work, this represents her recognition of the fact that, while we may feel stigmatized by our divorce, we are all nevertheless persons whose worth and competence are not totally defined by our marital relationships.

Once recognized, these become the beginning steps in the pattern of personal growth—the accretion of small changes in our everyday lives which we internalize and come to accept as definitions of what we are. They may seem so banal that we overlook them, but it is their very ordinariness that makes them so important. They remind us daily that there is hope, that we can survive on our own, that we are not helpless victims of our environment. Each of these seeds beneath the snow proves that our actions, our pleasures, our feelings—and therefore our selves—need not be defined by the relationship with our former spouse.

Cultivate them. They are harbingers of a greener season when you feel secure and comfortable as a single person. They will not flower overnight, in spite of what we hear from Madison Avenue. I find the reality of change best expressed by the psychologist Carl Rogers in a quote I keep posted on my refrigerator door:

Many people seem to feel that change in one's self-concept can come about smoothly. This is not true in any person. . . . When we learn something significant about our selves and act on that new learning, that starts a wave of consequences we can never fully anticipate.

For even the recently separated or divorced person, the healing process of change has already begun. In a hundred small ways you are acting, feeling, and thinking differently from the way you were before. Turning these changes into personal growth means, first, becoming aware of their existence, second, acknowledging their significance, and, finally, assuming the responsibility for the direction in which they will move your life. Each of us has this freedom to control our lives—and the responsibility that goes with it. For the divorced or separated person the freedom is greater, but so is the responsibility. No one can accept it for you; it is yours alone.

Subsequent chapters of this book set forth the guidelines for each stage of the creative divorce process, and examine the promises and pitfalls each stage holds. Behind my words are the experiences of the hundreds of men and women I have learned from in my seminars. Theirs is the best evidence that the challenge of change is well worth accepting.

CHAPTER 2

Coming to Terms
with Your Past Marriage

THE PULL
OF THE PAST

Divorce does not automatically end a marital relationship. Years of emotional and sexual closeness, mutual dependencies, and ingrained habits of living, loving, and hating together have created bonds too strong for a divorce decree to sever with a single stroke. On the surface this seems logical enough. Yet I have found that, among all the dilemmas divorce poses, the power of the past is the hardest to understand and, once understood, the most difficult to overcome.

Conventional wisdom permits only the abandoned spouse to yearn for the lost marriage. The rest of us are supposed to feel unalleviated joy, or at least the quiet satisfaction that comes from having made a painful but necessary decision. In truth, however, no divorced man or woman is immediately free from the past—neither the abandoned, the abandoners, nor those whose parting was mutual. For most of us, marriage provided the closest bond with a member of the opposite sex, apart from our mothers or fathers, that we have ever known. To assume that by establishing separate households we can instantaneously end this relationship is to deny the very deep

51

emotional needs which it satisfied, however perversely, and the degree to which it shaped our identities.

It would be foolish to claim that we will ever regard our former mate as just another person in our lives, especially when that person is mother or father to our children. We all have, and need, our pasts; without a strong sense of personal history to give our present and future lives some shape, we would have to create a new reason for being every morning. Our marriage is part of this past, and too much of our selves was formed in that union for us ever to blot it out completely, even if we wanted to.

The problem for newly separated or divorced people is the disproportionate power of their pasts to twist their vision of the present into a repetition of what they left behind. Many embark on a single existence determined to be free of their marriage—to blot it out completely—but soon discover this to be legally, financially, and emotionally impossible. They can define only two alternatives, equally bleak: either a continuing bondage to a relationship which no longer exists in fact, or a complete break with their former mate. The first seems intolerable; the second, unattainable, and, if there are children, unrealistic.

Yet somewhere between total emotional neutrality and immobilizing emotional entanglement there is a point at which each person can strike a balance he or she can live with comfortably. Through the creative divorce process you can lay the past to rest, and keep it from being the major influence over your present and your future. You can come to appreciate those aspects of your past marriage which enhanced a positive self-image. You can maintain those contacts with your former mate which circumstances may require without fearing a lifetime of emotional turmoil which initial meetings seem to foretell. You can, in short, keep the best from the past without sacrificing present independence and happiness or the possibility of rewarding new relationships in the future.

Granted, the process is neither easy nor automatic. At

the outset you may feel like a person who had thought he would cut a cable with a single swing of an axe, and instead is given a wire cutter and told to snip only certain strands. You may be so confused by your mixed feelings that you can't see where to begin cutting, or even be sure you want to. In one limited sense the abandoned spouse has it easier, in that he or she feels less initial ambivalence toward the past, and in the first months of separation longs unconditionally for the return of the absent mate—no matter the hostility that may fuel the yearning. More perplexing are the unforeseen emotional pushes and pulls that continue to dominate the lives of those who separated of their own volition. In many cases their divorce was an agonizing act of will which followed months or even years of indecision and misery. Having finally taken the step they thought would resolve things once and for all, they are shaken to discover that their feelings, thoughts, and actions are still in thrall to the past. In fact, they find they are devoting *more* thought, *more* energy, *more* emotional juices to their old relationship now than they did during many years of the marriage itself.

THE RECONFIRMATION EFFECT

Although the past seems to govern every moment in the lives of those going through the first months of separation, its power to seduce and destroy reaches a peak during meetings with the "practically former" spouse. How well I remember my own turmoil during those initial confrontations. Where once there were only two people, now I saw four: a man and woman suddenly strangers to ourselves and each other, and the familiar husband and wife we once had been. The room was crowded with memories of the past, and they seemed much more real than I felt my single self to be. These memories pushed between the lines of whatever business discussion had brought us together, summoning up the pleasant times, the small talk, the sexual attraction, the dependencies, the frustrations, the disappointments. The rational me knew that the marriage was ended, but my emotional self was not yet prepared to accept this fact.

Perhaps even more devastating than the internal fragmentation such meetings produce is the realization that in all probability we will have to go through them again and again and again. At such times it is only natural to feel like the young woman in one of my seminars who blurted out, "Sometimes I wish he were really dead, it would be so much simpler. He continues to make trouble, doesn't pay child support on time, calls up to criticize me and the way I'm handling the kids. I kick myself for not hanging up. It's as if we were still married."

These feelings are part of the necessary and painful process of pulling apart—of "hanging up" emotionally on our past relationship—which must take place before a new life can begin. Just because a relationship has ended in fact does not cancel the emotional needs it fulfilled, even if through hostility and anger. It is the fact that these needs are now unmet which gives rise to fond hopes for reunion and prevents us from letting go. By activating these hopes, meetings with a former mate provide the opportunity for us to test them against reality, and eventually to recognize them as fantasies born of emotional need which our past marriage can no longer satisfy. This is what I term the *reconfirmation effect,* the process by which our emotions accept the fact that the marriage is over.

Resistance at first is normal: in the initial stages of separation we feel totally cut off from the familiar routines and rituals of our married life—a life which now seems far more secure and fulfilling than the empty existences we have been thrown into. The reluctance to pull apart takes as many different forms as the complex of emotional needs which the marriage itself attempted to satisfy. When the separation was a mutual decision made by two people who pride themselves on being reasonable, it is often hidden under the guise of being civilized. "After all," a recently divorced teacher told me, "we still have common professional interests. Why shouldn't I call her up and tell her about something that happened at school? Why shouldn't we have an occasional dinner together? Can't we still be friends?" Yet when questioned further, he admitted that behind what he thought was an amicable professional relationship was his continuing need to know what she was doing and who she was spending her time with.

At the other extreme are those who devote their lives to the punishment of their former mate. They overlook no opportunity to pursue their marital battles during and after the divorce proceedings in a desperate attempt to perpetuate the hostility which gave the only meaning to their lives during the marriage. These are the people who run up enormous legal fees and then complain about the avariciousness of all lawyers. It does no good to tell them that a lawyer's time is money, and that an hour of haggling over a frying pan costs as much as an hour's discussion of a life insurance policy. They are lost in the pursuit of a self-destructive but peculiarly satisfying emotional relationship. It would be fortunate if they limited their wrangling to kitchen equipment; more often it is the children who are the victims.

Most divorced people fall somewhere in the middle of a spectrum between civilized self-delusion and all-consuming hatred. In spite of being hurt and angry, they are willing to try to be fair. They want to do the right thing by their former spouse and their children. They say their fondest wish is to let bygones be bygones, yet the best intentions vanish every time they must deal with their former mates. Try as they will, they can find no neutral ground. Every look, every "offhand" comment, every "casual" question carries an emotional charge, and before they know it they are off to the races again: Why can't he mind his own business? Why did she wear that dress? Why does he have to tell me who he's going out with? And why do I still care?

Quite often the emotional responses such meetings generate can surprise both partners. The long-suffering wife who sat on her anger during the marriage out of fear that it might drive her husband away (and besides, according to the rules of our culture women aren't supposed to express or even feel anger toward their husbands) becomes ferocious in the lawyer's office. She is shocked at her stubborn insistence that she get what's coming to her, and horrified that the depth and power of her hostility can erupt in such unladylike language. As one genteel matron confessed, "If somebody had told me two years ago that I would sit in a lawyer's office and call my husband a bastard, I wouldn't have believed it. I didn't even *think* words like that."

In the long run the honest expression of feelings is always healthier than the martyring techniques some men and women employ. Martyring assumes the position, "He/she has made me suffer desperately and I'm making sure he/she knows it. He/she will come back and then I'll make sure he/she knows what a monster he/she has been." Anger denied and guilt perpetuated are at the root of martyring. Many women live for Friday evening when the husband comes to pick up the children and can see his wife stoic in her grief. Women have no monopoly on this ploy: men are just as careful to let their former wives know in devious ways just how much they are suffering. "Look what you've done to me," they will say, although not in so many words. "It's all your fault that I lost my job, or caught the flu, or have to live in a furnished room."

At the farthest reaches of martyring are the letters threatening suicide. One distraught woman, divorced after twenty years of marriage, showed me a letter from her alcoholic husband in which he wrote he had been taking walks on the Golden Gate Bridge, and that if she didn't take him back he was going to jump. And it would be her fault. Rational? No, but fiendishly effective.

Martyring in whatever form plays on guilt, which stands as perhaps the greatest obstacle to breaking the pull of the past. Guilt, the invisible bond of so many marriages, can still exert a powerful pull after the marriage has ended. Like the woman whose ex-husband was an alcoholic, many men and women stuck out a bad marriage as long as they did because they could not tolerate the guilt that "abandoning" their mate would produce. Even when guilt was not an important bond in a marriage, it increases with a divorce or separation. Because it pervades the lives of almost all divorced people, guilt requires no overt act of martyring to be activated. Society sees to that. The husband who leaves an unhappy marriage is made to feel irresponsible, a philanderer (even if there was no "other woman"), a destroyer of the home. "My God," he will think, "I've abandoned her and she can never survive," or, "What will become of the kids now that I can't protect them against her?"

Women particularly are susceptible to feelings of guilt and failure stemming from unrealistically high demands society has placed on them in their roles as wife and mother. Wives are supposed to be the tenders of the hearth, the nurses of the fragile male ego, the ameliorators, the smoothers-over. Even when a husband abandons his wife for his mistress, she is still made to feel that the break-up is somehow her fault: it was something she did, or more often something she didn't do. If only she had been better in bed, kept the house cleaner, asserted herself less—or asserted herself more—the marriage would not have ended.

While in the first throes of separation we may not be able to recognize the irrationality of such feelings, we should be aware of their existence and understand their power to pull us back to the old relationship. Because our new lives may be so empty we will grasp at almost any excuse, no matter how self-destructive, to get back together. We tell ourselves that we have learned our lesson, we have both changed enough to try again and this time do it right. This hope sets off all kinds of rationalizations to set up a meeting for testing it out: trumped-up legal questions, extended discussions on the disposition of a particular chair, unnecessary phone calls to check on the children's welfare ("If you're going camping, remember to give Johnny his hayfever pills"), and proffers of assistance ("Do you need help with the storm windows?").

SOME FIRST-AID MEASURES
CAN START A LASTING CURE

Illusions arising from emotional need die hard. We can use the necessary meetings with our former mate to help lay them to rest—if we understand the process. If we don't, time will eventually cover things over but the healing process will be longer and more agonizing than need be. We can stand only so much suffering; eventually we must live or die. Years later we may wonder how we could ever have "let ourselves" endure such agony.

How our wounds heal is up to us. If we simply sit back and trust to time, it may close them over on the surface with an ugly scar trapping deep within us permanent infection that will poison our lives and our attitudes to other people in ways we may never recognize. However, if we seize the opportunity for personal growth in even these initial confrontations, we can set in motion a cure which is likely to be more lasting and complete. The following guidelines will not turn these meetings into pleasant social get-togethers, but they do suggest how you can use them to discover, test, and strengthen internal resources that have been dormant until now.

1. *Stick to business.* Easier said than done, but you have means at your disposal to make it possible. First ask yourself, "Is this meeting really necessary, or could matters be handled with greater dispatch by telephone or letter or through the lawyers?" If a meeting is indeed called for, be sure you have a firm grasp on its purpose and have thought through your position. When negotiation is involved—over finances, for example, or child visitation rights—don't assume you will necessarily reach agreement at once, or that you have to settle things on the spot. Remember how long it takes even the most skillful labor negotiator or international diplomat to work out details of an agreement both sides can accept.

If you seem to have reached an impasse in one of these meetings, stop. Don't give in just to "get it over with," or you may find yourself stuck with an arrangement you will live to regret. Many divorced people have found that postponing settlement of those irreconcilable issues which can be put off—and taking temporary action on those which cannot—makes it easier later on to work out final and binding agreements both parties can live with comfortably. When the smoke clears and feelings cool off, many sticking points dissolve in the recognition that they were really efforts to "get" the other spouse and not necessary conditions to future well-being. If you can keep punitive measures out of final decisions, it will be easier to get off your marital treadmill of guilt and blame, and start living your new life.

When you do manage to get through the items on the agenda—or see that they require further time—don't start on any new business. If you couldn't reach agreement on the problem you got together to solve, neither of you is probably in any condition to deal rationally with other affairs. The "as-long-as-I'm-here-why-don't-we-talk-about-summer-vacations" gambit is not likely to prove very productive under the circumstances. Furthermore, it is unfair to your former spouse, who may not have had the opportunity to give much coherent thought to the subject.

Accept the fact that stilted conversation and awkward silences are inevitable in these meetings; unpleasant as they are, attempts to smooth them over can needlessly ignite emotional conflagrations which will reduce you both to cinders, and keep the business at hand from being resolved. "I saw that new Italian film the other evening," a husband may say by way of making pleasant chitchat to reduce the tension. "I hope you enjoyed it!" the wife may lash back. "Maybe if you sent your checks on time I could afford a baby-sitter and get out of the house myself once in a while!" "Oh, for God's sake," he responds, "can't you ever stop nagging?"—and they are off again, round and round the well-worn track of their old marital races.

Be aware, too, that asking "innocent" questions in a highly charged emotional atmosphere can be just as inflammatory as volunteering unnecessary information. "Have you had lunch with Jim Borden recently?" a wife may inquire of her husband while they are sitting in the lawyer's reception room. "No, why?" he counters testily. "Has Janet been giving you an earful about me?" The legal questions the meeting was called to clarify will now be clouded by the emotional turmoil this interchange has stirred up, and both will be busy with the unspoken thoughts racing in their heads. He: Why can't she mind her own business? Don't I deserve a life of my own? My lawyer will maker her suffer. She: He must be carrying on with somebody for him to be so touchy. I knew it wouldn't take long. He never loved me. My lawyer will make him suffer.

Obviously, you cannot avoid the automatic exchanges which grease the wheels of everyday social interaction, but be alert to their capacity to set off barely controlled emotions. Even "how are you?" can explode in your face. In any event it is not likely to elicit an answer to your liking.

"Fine" probably isn't true, and if it were you wouldn't want to hear it—any more than you are prepared to deal with "I'm miserable, thank you." But if you can keep extraneous questions to a minimum, you stand a better chance of staying on firm ground and avoiding the emotional soft shoulders which keep you from the problem at hand.

2. *Be alert to double signals.* It is only natural that you both are sending out double signals, since you both are ambivalent in your feelings toward each other. You may have thought you arrived at a decision to call it quits, but your life since the separation may have been so miserable you are having second thoughts, conscious or unconscious. Even if you think you never want to see your ex-spouse again, you suddenly find yourself getting ready for a meeting as if you were going out on a date, or cleaning up the house and buying fresh flowers for the living room.

You may think that by wearing a new suit or getting your hair done you are showing your former mate that you are functioning capably in your single state. This may be true. There is certainly no reason not to look as good as you can. Clothes may not make the man, but they can help build his self-esteem. Many men and women get a lift in the first months of separation from a new hairstyle or new kinds of clothes which depart dramatically from their old "married" images.

Remember, however, that these externals are likely to be misread by your former spouse—or, more accurately, that you both may see only those signals you choose to see. Don't be surprised if he or she picks up signals of attraction which you may be half-consciously sending out as well. Obviously, attracting signals do not depend on a new hairdo or suit—in fact, a remembered dress or after-shave scent can prove far more devastating, and the familiar combination of gesture, voice, and movement of your former mate by itself cannot help but revive powerful memories of past happiness.

It is clearly this continuing ability of your former spouse, by his or her very existence, to rekindle these feelings that makes meetings so painful. There is little either of you can do to stifle completely the ambivalence they engender. You can, however, examine the motivation behind behavior which may needlessly compound matters. One woman whose husband had never spent much time on his appearance during the marriage was thrown when he came to every postmarital meeting freshly shaved and talcumed in a dark suit and fashionable tie. "I couldn't figure it out," she said. "Was he trying to tell me he had changed and wanted me to take him back, or was it more like, 'Look what you're missing out on now, baby'? After every meeting I got furious."

The immediate answer to her question, in all probability, was both, although the husband may not have realized what he was doing. However, the net effect was to make the wife angry—at her husband for making himself attractive to her, and at herself for responding. Her solution lay not in trying to decide what his motivations were, but in using her anger to help pull her apart from the old relationship, to recognize that in spite of conflicting signals the marriage was over. Subsequent meetings would then be easier—not much, but a little.

3. *Avoid judgment words.* In spite of the objective fact that no one person is "guilty" of breaking up a marriage, in the initial stages of separation both parties are more than willing to cast or accept blame. Words like "should" or "ought," seemingly harmless questions beginning "Why did you . . ." or even "helpful" advice can trigger angry feelings lurking just beneath our self-control. The subject need not be the marriage; even a passing comment on room decor or child care can be taken as implied criticism:

He: Shouldn't he be wearing his playclothes? He won't be

able to have much fun in the park if he has to wear his good suit.

She: How am I supposed to know you're taking him to the park if you don't tell me?

He: I told you last weekend. You never did listen to anything I ever said!

She: You did not tell me! And now you're trying to blame me for forgetting! It's no wonder I worry every time you take him out. You can't be trusted.

And so an "innocent" question has resurrected a past marital battle in which guilt was assigned and punishment handed down. What could have been an actual misunderstanding has turned into an instant replay of past behavior which defined the marriage: all she can see in him is the same irresponsible person she had tried unsuccessfully to change during the marriage. To him, she is still the same hyper-critical nag.

The sooner you can turn off the blame-making machinery of your former marriage, the sooner you can reclaim a sense of your own worth. If the wounds of your break-up are too fresh for you to forgive and forget, you can at least try to avoid those first shots which always seem to lead to full-scale warfare. Continued attempts to downgrade your spouse—or yourself—serve no purpose except to damage the self-esteem you both need to function as independent people.

4. *Respect your former mate's independence and don't hesitate to stand up for your own.* No matter how curious you may be about your former spouse's life, it is none of your concern—nor should you sit still for inordinate prying into your own affairs. Mild curiosity is normal, but when you find yourself spending a lot of emotional energy worrying about what he or she is doing (or going out of your way to keep your activities secret from him or her) you are still tied to the past.

This bond can explain a great deal of needless anxiety—

and some "freakish" coincidences as well. One woman said that every time her ex-husband came to pick up the children he found some excuse to wander into the kitchen and cast his eyes over her appointment book next to the telephone. "I found myself emptying ashtrays before he came over so he wouldn't get suspicious and start asking questions. I stopped doing that the day a friend of mine told me I was behaving exactly like a guilty wife. Why should I worry about what he thinks? We're not married any more. I notice he still checks out my date book, but that's his hang-up, not mine."

Another woman claimed that she "always" seemed to run into her ex-husband. He was everywhere—in the supermarket, at the bank, pulled up next to her car at the stoplight—and she said she was getting afraid to go out of the house. The other members of the group saw through to the fact (which she had not recognized) that she *wanted* to meet him and was unconsciously acting on her knowledge of his daily schedule to make sure she would be wherever he was likely to turn up. She didn't have to stay home to avoid him; once she decided that she wanted to avoid him, it was a simple matter to adjust her daily routine.

Recognizing the fact that the two of you are now separate people often requires an act of self-assertion you may not feel to be necessary. A wife, for example, may reject her husband's offer of a separate lawyer to represent her in the divorce proceedings on the pretext that it would be "too expensive." What she is really doing is denying the fact of her own independence, and that her interests have diverged from her husband's. Having her own lawyer stands as evidence that she is now indeed a single person and as such has rights which the law will protect.

Sometimes—as in the case of the woman whose ex-husband kept her on the phone while he criticized her performance as a mother—simply hanging up can be an effective solution to a practical problem and a significant step toward independence as well. In other instances we can demonstrate independence by rejecting an offer of assistance which may have been extended with the best intentions. This may be the first summer of your divorce and your wife may have never had to worry about installing the air conditioners, but that's her problem now. If she turns down your suggestion to drop over and install them for her, try to accept her decision as a healthy sign that she is making the effort to go it alone—galling as it may be to realize that she can take care of herself without you.

5. *Examine expressions of disinterested friendship from (or toward) your spouse.* In my experience, almost every person who takes pride in continued close friendship and frequent social contact with a former spouse in the initial stages of separation is playing an elaborate game of self-delusion. Sometimes both spouses, unable to accept the anger each feels toward the other, cover it over with protestations of "of course, we're still very good friends." Such sophistication may be the envy of their social set, but they are nevertheless denying the very real emotional forces which propelled them toward divorce in the first place. (And their carefully watched pot may boil over when one hears that the other is having a delightful affair with a new person.)

More common are the husbands and wives whose single lives are so barren, meaningless, and uncertain that they drift back to each other simply because they have not been able to find anything better. In comparison with their present emptiness, even old hostilities are comforting: the devil I know scares me less than the devil I don't know. Despite the rationalizations employed to deny the real motivating loneliness (he hasn't had a decent meal in three weeks, it's good for the children, I've got an extra ticket), these are dead-end affairs. Each partner is stuck with one foot firmly planted on the shores of the past, and the other poised just above the waters of the present. Until one or the other makes a move, both are frozen in illusion. They are no longer husband and wife, they can never be brother and sister, and chances are slim, especially at first, that they are really good friends.

The hollowness of such "friendship" is amply demonstrated in the experience of a woman whose former husband had insisted on a clause in the divorce that permitted him to spend Christmas with her and the children. "The first Christmas was awful. He sat at the head of the table, just like he used to, but it wasn't the same. We were living a kind of lie. I couldn't sit there as if I were still his wife, so I made up excuses to stay in the kitchen. The next year I fixed a buffet so we could spread out and he could eat in the living room with the children, but if I could do it over I wouldn't have him there at all."

I am not advocating all-out war, nor do I underestimate the internal well-being that comes with eventually being able to say (and to feel), "Yes, I can see that my former mate is not a monster. We are very different, but we are both persons of value." What I do claim, on the basis of my own experience, is that this eminently desirable goal is an end-product of the creative divorce process, not its beginning consequence. This is not to deny the very real generous and positive feelings we may have toward our former mate, even in the first months of separation. We should not, however, blind ourselves to the self-victimizing purposes to which we can put these feelings. Our capacity at this stage to deny or rationalize away equally strong feelings of hatred, resentment, and hostility is almost infinite. In the beginning our emotions are too contradictory to permit much objectivity, and before we congratulate ourselves on being so civilized, we should check to make sure that we have not fallen into a subtle trap of our own making which prevents us from striking out on our own.

Only when you feel secure as an independent person can you be certain that expressions of friendship toward your former mate are really friendly feelings and not unrecognized hangovers of emotional need from the past marriage. Until you reach this point, it is far better to accept whatever anger and hostility caused you to separate in the first place and use them to pull apart from the old relationship and set about beginning your new life as a single person.

One of the most seductive attractions of contacts with former mates is their power to impose some structure, if only fleetingly, on what seem otherwise totally chaotic existences. If only we could make sense out of what was happening to us, we wouldn't need the support that keeps drawing us back to the old relationship. There is a pattern in this chaos: it is the pattern of mourning. The next chapter examines the healing process of mourning and sets forth guidelines for making this experience healthy and constructive.

CHAPTER 3

The Healing Process of Mourning

SEPARATION SHOCK

One of the reasons Helen gave for enrolling in my divorce adjustment group was a description of the seminar she saw in her local newspaper which included the phrase "death of a relationship."

"That really hit me when I read it," she said at the second session. "I had been sitting in the kitchen with the help-wanted ads for most of the morning—staring at a pile of dirty laundry and trying to decide if I should wash the clothes or look for a job. They both seemed equally important—and equally meaningless. I simply couldn't work up the energy to do one or the other, and when I saw those words, 'death of a relationship,' I suddenly realized that's exactly how I felt, as if part of me were dead. Since Bob left I had been walking around the house like a zombie; I hardly slept or ate or went out of the house if I didn't absolutely have to. Food had no taste. Except for a stomachache that wouldn't go away, I felt numb, as if someone had shot me full of Novocain. I could see the real world, but it was way off there somewhere in the distance."

She went no further, suddenly embarrassed at having revealed so much of her real feelings to a group of almost total strangers. There was a long moment of silence. Then a man said, "I know exactly what you mean. I felt the same way! When we split up, it was as if the clock had stopped. I used to cancel appointments and just sit in my office with the door closed. I didn't accept or return any calls. Once a secretary came in and found me weeping—not making any noise, just tears streaming down my face. She must have thought I was crazy. I know I did."

Another woman who had been listening intently said, "When my husband left, the house became my tomb—not a grave, more like a pyramid full of relics. Sometimes I felt like a mummy and at other times it seemed as if I were supposed to be the caretaker. He had left his bathrobe hanging on a hook in the closet and I couldn't decide what to do with it. Should I leave it there, pack it away, send it to him, throw it out? It's still hanging there."

At times like this I can almost hear clicks of recognition inside the members of the group when they realize that other people going through a divorce or separation have experienced feelings similar to their own. It is a tremendous relief for them when they learn that the images of death, graves, and life-in-suspension that pre-occupy their thoughts are not signs of extreme morbidity, but typical to many others in the same predicament. "I really thought I was going insane," a fifty-year-old woman confessed. "There was an invisible shield between me and the rest of the world that I couldn't break through. Nothing was familiar to me any more. People on the streets looked like robots. Even the faces of old friends seemed somehow different. I felt cut off from everything."

These and other similar reactions, common to newly divorced or separated people, are symptoms of what I call *separation shock* which a divorce or separation can produce. The longer and more involving the marriage, the greater the severity of these symptoms, and the more extensive their spread throughout our lives. When we have invested a major portion of our time and energies in a relationship, its ending can radiate waves of depression, hostility, self-pity, guilt, remorse, anxiety, and fear too conflicting to comprehend, and too powerful to cope with immediately. They can poison everything: food tastes like sand, normal chores defeat us, new problems loom everywhere, and we wonder why we should get up in the morning at all.

The degree to which a separation or divorce can produce these reactions is in direct proportion to the part the marriage played in shaping our identities. For most of us marriage was the primary determiner of ourselves: it told us who we were, what to do, how to behave towards others, what to feel. It supplied the reasons for living and the rules by which we lived, although we may not have realized all this while we were married. For many of us, it is the only kind of life we can remember with any vividness. Even those men who had always thought of themselves as relatively independent, self-sufficient people are stunned at an internal void which opens inside them once they begin living alone. As one man, separated for six months, reported in a shaking voice, "I always considered myself a pretty independent guy. I have a staff of six under me at work and they know I'm the boss. But now I don't know what's the matter. I never realized how much I miss my kids, and my old house, and even the arguments with my wife. I feel like I'm falling apart inside."

Next to the death of a loved one, most of us find divorce to be the almost traumatic experience in our lives. When we consider that we refer to our mates as "my life," "my right hand," or "my better half," we should not be surprised that separation from that mate produces reactions in many ways identical to those which an actual death can set in motion. Divorce is indeed a death—a death of a relationship; and just as the death of someone close to us brings on a period of mourning during which we come to terms with our loss, so too a marital break-up is followed by a similar period of mourning. If we can come to recognize, accept, and live through the conflicting emotions which are part of the mourning process, it can become an important stage of our personal growth into independent people. Without an understanding of what this process means, we are likely to remain mired in the past—wallowing in self-pity, cursing our former mate, idealizing our lost marriage—or, if we do emerge, we may sustain permanent scars. Americans have paid little attention to how people mourn. We have instead pushed the entire experience into the same dim recesses of oblivion where, until recently, we relegated the whole question of death and dying. We grudgingly grant the fact of death, but do our very best to deny its processes or its impact on the survivors. And we do the same with divorce.

Such denial is dangerous. Mourning will take place in any event; if denied or suppressed, however, its healing powers will not be effectively utilized. To restore physiological and emotional balance we must accept all the feelings engendered by a loss. These are not always pleasant feelings. In even the most loving relationship, loss will produce in the survivor strong hostility toward the one who has left. Rationally this may not make sense; emotionally, we feel abandoned. We feel guilty over real or imagined instances of acts performed or not performed during the past, knowing they can never be set to rights now. These feelings are produced in the most harmonious relationship. In an ambivalent union characterized by large components of love *and* hate, attraction *and* fear, dependency *and* resentment, the negative emotions the survivor experiences—together with the loss of the familiar role and habits of being husband or wife—may prove too terrifying to recognize or accept. He or she then retreats to fantasies in which the absent partner is still present and life is as it was before.

The mourning process provides a way for us to ventilate all these conflicting feelings—a ventilation for our growth into independent persons. Its effect is to heal our psychic wounds so that we can then free ourselves from entrapment in the past and start the process of living constructively in the present.

THE PATTERN BEHIND THE MOURNING PROCESS: HELEN'S STORY (II)

Every person going through a divorce or separation experiences a unique mix of these conflicting feelings. They are normal aspects of the mourning that follows the death of a relationship. We all attempt to deny the reality of the fact that the marriage has ended. We all feel conflicting surges of nostalgia for and anger against our former mates and our past marriages. We all feel that our present lives have lost much of their savor. Helen's story, while unique to her, demonstrates how these internal reactions become manifest in everyday life. From her experience we can discern the pattern behind what seems at first to be chaos, and learn to spot the promises and pitfalls for personal growth the pattern holds for us.

"I think the separation would be easier to take if it hadn't come at the same time a lot of other things were going wrong," Helen said. "In fact, ever since Bob left, my whole life has taken a turn for the worse. It's enough to make you believe in astrology. First the doctor says that Jimmy is going to have to wear special shoes for a while to correct a back problem he's been having. Then I get a letter from the day camp telling me I didn't send in the deposit on time and that the kids have been put on the waiting list. If they don't get in this summer, that means I never will be able to work. And can you believe the exterminator discovered dry rot in the back porch? If it weren't so sad, I could almost laugh. Meanwhile, here I am trying to be mother *and* father *and* head of the house."

Helen blames her husband for much of her present unhappiness. "Take the dry rot. If he had paid half as much attention to his responsibilities around the house as he did to his golf swing, it would never have gotten out of hand. I was always the one who ended up getting things fixed. And wouldn't you know he's suddenly become the big-time father?" she continued, her voice rising in anger and her face flushing. "Last Sunday he didn't get the kids home until 9:30 at night—dirty and hungry, of course—and Nancy is only eight. God only knows what they had been doing, but she was so tired she threw a tantrum right in the hallway. And he had the nerve to say, 'Gee, I don't know what's wrong with her. She was perfectly fine all weekend.' I was so furious at him I cried for two hours after he left. Actually, I don't know why I get so upset by this kind of insensitivity. What else can you expect from a man?"

The reactions of Helen's friends, and her own changes in attitude toward them, represent another puzzling development that has added to her sense of hurt and isolation. "I get the strong impression I'm some kind of pariah. The other day I was at the store and spotted the mother of one of Jimmy's classmates, whom I had gotten to know through the PTA. She actually ducked behind a display of gardening equipment to avoid having to talk to me. It's getting to be a pattern. This town is like Noah's Ark: if you aren't part of a pair, they shut you out.

"I can take snubs from acquaintances, but even women I have been close friends with for years seem to be giving me the cold shoulder. I guess it shouldn't surprise me, considering the mess I've made of my life. I will say that my next-door neighbor has gone out of her way to be nice. We still get together once or twice a week for coffee in the morning. She tries to understand and say the right thing, but how can I expect her to know what the right thing is when I don't know it myself? Then I remember that she can go back to her husband, while I'm stuck here by myself, and that gets me depressed.

"The worst experience was with Betty, a good friend of

mine who's been divorced for years and claims she has sworn off men completely. She and Bob never liked each other much; she always claimed he was holding me back. You'd think I'd really want to see her, wouldn't you, so that we could swap stories on the evils of all men? Well, for some reason I didn't tell Betty about the separation and when she heard about it from somebody else she called me up, furious that I hadn't confided in her. I told her I knew what she would say and I didn't want to hear it. We've patched things up since, but our friendship hasn't been as close as it was before. She's still trying to get me back in the world—helping with my resumé, and suggesting jobs I should apply for. I can see the logic in what she says, but I keep resisting her. Doesn't make much sense, does it?"

Helen feels that because of these experiences she is spending more and more time by herself. "It's getting so I prefer my solitude, lonely as it is. Last night I stayed up until three o'clock trying to sort out in my mind just where things went wrong. I even tried writing down a list of the main points, but I haven't got it straight yet."

What's going on here? Helen suspects that she is caught up in a string of bad luck. Is she also on her way to becoming a bitter, man-hating recluse? Has her breakup exposed a basic inability to function independently which her marriage had always kept hidden—and if so, should she find a new husband as quickly as possible who can provide the support she seems to require? Or would it be better for her to follow what she thinks is Betty's advice: carve out a totally involving career for herself and thus avoid the temptation to fall into a new relationship which will eventually only cause her more hurt and pain?

Before making any final evaluation of Helen's future, let's consider the elements of her present story and examine what they reveal about the process of mourning she is going through now.

"MY WHOLE LIFE HAS TAKEN
A TURN FOR THE WORSE . . ."

Without question Helen now faces new problems that she did not have as a married woman. There are the economic facts of life that she will probably have to get a job, that even so she will be living on a reduced income, and that her salary will be taxed according to a higher rate than if she were married. Working all day will mean that she will have to adjust her schedule to allow for the increased responsibilities she now bears. She is indeed mother and father and head of the house now, and must somehow expand her day to include shopping, working, housekeeping, children, and enough time for a private social life. At first she may feel like the young divorced mother who said, "My life is a series of spinning plates. One false move and they all shatter. If the baby-sitter calls up sick at the last minute, I can't go to work and my whole routine is thrown off. I never knew just getting through twenty-four hours took so much planning. I've got to decide three days in advance when to wash my hair."

The practical realities can be equally as difficult for men. Along with the overtones of rejection and demasculinization which get in the way of cooking, cleaning, and picking up after themselves, most men have little idea of how to perform domestic chores—and no concept at all of the complicated logistics necessary to a smoothly running household. Although at the beginning they might prefer to pay for domestic service, most cannot afford servants or constant restaurant bills. They too are living on a reduced income. Their salaries are also taxed at a higher rate. And they are chagrined to learn that while alimony (or spousal support, as it is now called in some states) is tax deductible, child support is not. Many ex-husbands who had considered themselves free of male chauvinism become furious when their ex-wives stand on the principle of total liberation and insist that money from their husbands be designated child support and not spousal support. To these women, alimony is a symbol of continued dependence; to the men it's a smart tax move. For both, it's a real problem.

Helen touched on another real problem when she said, "This town's like Noah's Ark: if you aren't part of a pair, they shut you out." Although in this context the remark is an overreaction to a specific situation (more about this later), there is considerable truth in what she said. If her town is like most suburbs, it probably is designed for couples. Undoubtedly it was this aspect which proved especially attractive during her marriage: a harmonious combination of school, social, and family activities revolving around the institution of marriage. Her married days were totally compatible with this pattern. When Helen begins to get out in the world, she will find out that this same pattern pervades the culture. "Married" is normal, beyond a certain age. "Single" is not. She will learn, just as men do, that her marital status is important to a potential employer, and that by checking off "divorced" on a job application she may have reduced her chances for getting hired. As a single woman she will often be denied credit. She may have to threaten legal action to get long-standing charge accounts transferred to her own name, or else go through the humiliating experience of having her ex-husband vouch for her reliability. Although these and other examples of discrimination against single women are slowly passing from the scene, thanks in large part to the persistent efforts of the women's movement, they are still prevalent and very real.

But: What does Helen mean when she says her life has taken a turn for the worse since her husband left? As evidence she offers the dry rot, Jimmy's corrective shoes, and the chance that her children may not get into day camp.

Yet when viewed objectively, these appear to be no more than the kinds of normal minor crisis that can be expected to complicate daily life from time to time. Two of these—Jimmy's back and the dry rot—had been in the making since before her husband's departure. Furthermore, as Helen herself admitted, she was always the one who had to take charge of household repairs. Why should she now be overwhelmed by these events? And why should she link them to her separation?

Part of the answer lies in Helen's tunnel vision. Like many other people in the initial stages of separation, Helen sees the entire world through the filter of her emotional pain. Because her separation absorbs practically all her thought and emotional energy, she interprets everything as a reflection of her internal state and therefore somehow connected. Where once she could keep problems compartmentalized and separate in her mind, now her problem-solving machinery is awash in the emotional turmoil her separation has stirred up. The only things Helen tells us about her life are the problems she must cope with, although there may well have been some pleasant and positive events which she neglected to include because they didn't seem worth mentioning—or because she blotted out their existence.

However, there is more at work here than just a superficial sourness toward life that turns us all into temporary pessimists at one time or another. At a deeper level, Helen *has* to feel helpless, she *has* to feel that she is incapable of taking care of herself as a single woman. To feel otherwise would be to repudiate her belief that her identity lay only in being a wife, to deny the precepts of marriage which hold that women are dependent and helpless. For her to deny their validity she would also have to deny the value of the sacrifices in personal independence and expressions of selfhood which she made in order to live according to her rules of married life. She is not yet emotionally prepared to make this judgment, so she unconsciously seeks out proof to show herself that she actually is incompetent and helpless as a single woman. Even normal functions that formed the pattern of her daily life now provide her with the opportunity to prove to herself that she cannot be that which she does not yet want to be: a single woman.

Helen's feelings at this stage are normal; she has not yet had time to develop a new self-image as a single person. She is protecting herself from the anxiety and disorientation that would ensue if she admitted she were no longer a married woman. Until she can put together an image of herself as a single person, she will go on viewing events from the vantage point of a married woman. Since her marriage directly or indirectly defined every part of her life, she will continue to interpret apparently unrelated problems as outgrowths of that lost relationship.

It is during times like these that separated or divorced people are shaken by how much of what they had thought was their independent identities had been bound up in their marital relationship. They suddenly feel that no longer being a husband or wife (especially if they have filled those roles for many years) means also no longer being a person. "Who am I now?" they cry. Small wonder that even the smallest chores that were once routine—repairing the dry rot, fixing the TV set—turn into reminders of undefined selves too harsh to face up to. In the initial stages of separation, it is normal and healthy to resist taking action which we feel would completely destroy whatever sense of ourselves we have left. The damage we would do to our emotional stability under these circumstances would be too great to sustain. Before we can let go of one identity, we must begin creating another to take its place.

Greater security in being a single person will come with time: it cannot come overnight. The danger lies in remaining in this transitional period so long that the necessary pause to gather internal strength turns into a trap of inactivity and helplessness. Every small step we take during this period to master what seems to be a hostile environment helps prove that perhaps it isn't so hostile and monolithic as we had thought. If we continue to seek out evidence that the world is conspiring against us, we will overlook opportunities we have at hand to assume—more accurately, resume—control. Take problems one at a time. In Helen's case, for instance, none of her crises is, by itself, insurmountable, once she perceives them as separate situations and not points on a giant iceberg. By taking them one by one, she stands a greater chance of solving some of them than if she persists in her all-or-nothing attitude. As she no doubt did during her married life, she may have to establish priorities, since she does in fact face many new and very real problems. The back porch may have to wait to get repaired until she can see to Jimmy's shoes or make other arrangements for the children's summer. Each solution will help diminish the influence of outside events, and increase her sense of being in control. As her world begins to resume its normal shape, she will be in a better position to deal with the real problems of living singly.

"FOR SOME REASON I DIDN'T TELL BETTY ABOUT THE SEPARATION. . . ."

Helen was aware of Betty's marital disaster, and of her attitudes toward men. She also knew what her friend thought of her husband. She therefore had a pretty good idea of what Betty's response to news of her separation would be—congratulations, why didn't you do it sooner, I told you he was no good, now you can get out of your rut—and she didn't want to hear it. Since Helen herself had moments when she entertained much the same opinions, the only explanation she could offer for not calling Betty was her general unhappiness and need to be left alone. When she understood the real reason behind her reluctance to talk with her friend, other pieces of behavior during the past two months began to fall into place, and she no longer felt in danger of cutting herself off permanently from the rest of the world.

By not telling Betty about the separation, Helen was acting on an unconscious but very strong emotional need to deny the fact that her marriage had ended. Even though part of her acknowledged the truth (the part that was looking through the help-wanted ads) her emotions were not yet ready to accept the fact. Not calling Betty was an unrecognized act of emotional self-preservation: Helen simply was not ready to fall in with Betty's only-too-eager willingness to consign the marriage to ancient history and help Helen get on with her new life. When Betty forced the issue by calling *her*, Helen lashed out in anger and cut off anything Betty had been about to say.

At this stage of her separation, Helen's reluctance to admit that her marriage has ended is quite normal and, as long as it does not continue to be the dominant force in her life, can work in her behalf. Denial is a normal and necessary human reaction to a crisis which is too immediately overwhelming to face head-on. Denial provides time for a temporary retreat from reality while our internal forces regroup and regain the strength to comprehend the new life our loss has forced upon us. During this time we withdraw into fantasies in which the loss has not occurred, and the absent person is still with us. In an effort to regain the lost person, we become preoccupied with the past in dreams and reverie. The more barren and frightening our present lives, the greater the appeal of a fantasy life.

Through our fantasies we review the past and internalize an image of it which will remain forever in our memory. During these times we should cherish the pleasant memories and recognize the positive contributions our former marriage made to our self-image, but we should also guard against an often pathetically eager willingness to accept fantasies as truth. If we let them dominate our present lives ("She'll stop that eternal nagging now that

I've shown her I won't take it any longer," or "He'll come home now that he sees how much he needs me"), we are guaranteeing ourselves nothing but more disappointment.

Denial permits us to test the reality of our new situation in pieces, absorbing only those aspects which do not threaten to destroy us completely. For most of us, reality eventually wins over; we come, slowly, to see our fantasies as just exactly that. Gradually we accept the fact that the relationship has ended, and that we now are single people. We all go through denial in one form or another when our marriage ends. Helen's story contains examples of denial which many recently divorced or separated people have also reported. Denial is at the root of her unwillingness to sleep in her marriage bed. The memories of that room are too powerful for her to accept at this point, so she shuts them off temporarily by sleeping in a guest bedroom until she has gained enough emotional strength to face them. It is also in part denial which keeps her suspended in the kitchen between the dirty clothes and the help-wanted ads. In spite of her recognition that she must now find work, she is unable to set about job hunting with any degree of interest until she can come to emotional terms with the fact that her marriage is over. Looking for a job is tangible proof of her single state which is too threatening at this stage of her separation to deal with effectively.

Each person must find his own schedule. When the time is right, there are steps you can take that will indicate that you are moving through the process of denial and that it need no longer dominate your life. Often these are relatively minor acts of self-assertion which, when recognized, become symbolic closings on the past. The woman who couldn't decide what to do with her husband's bathrobe demonstrates how she moved through denial into the present: "I'd been avoiding dusting the desk in the bedroom because I didn't want to disturb all my husband's papers that had been sitting there ever since he left. I guess I thought the marriage would be finished once and for all if I moved his things. But one day I forced myself to straighten up the desk, and once I got started I cleaned the whole thing out. Then I took his clothes out of the closet—including the bathrobe—and put them in the basement. Then I had a really good cry and felt better—not great, but the way you do when you get a hard job over with."

... SHE CONTINUED, HER VOICE RISING IN ANGER ...

Typically, Helen's story does not contain any explicit expressions of anger or resentment toward her husband for having left her. We can only sense it in her rising voice and flushed face when she relives in her emotions what happened when he brought the children back late one Sunday evening. As unthinking as his behavior may have been, we can assume it is probably familiar enough to Helen and that under normal circumstances it would not have triggered such a severe overreaction on her part. Yet, in the present context, she is reduced to tears of frustration and rage. Clearly, there must be an additional reason for her anger which she has not recognized.

The reason lies beneath the surface of conscious thought. Irrational as it appears, the departure from our lives of one who provided physical and emotional care inevitably produces intense feelings of anger toward that person for having left—even a man or woman who leaves a marriage of his own free will has these feelings. Their irrationality is further indicated by the fact that they strike even those who lose a close relative or friend through death. Mixed with sorrow and longing for the return of the dead person is extreme rage over having been abandoned by him or her. "How dare he die on me!" is the survivor's reaction. "How dare he leave me to this miserable life!" Because these feelings are so hostile and intense, and because we cannot logically account for their existence, we often deny them. We couldn't be feeling that way, it doesn't make any sense! If death can arouse such hostile emotions, how much stronger and more unacceptable are the anger and hostility which a marital break-up can call forth.

Denying these feelings does not cause them to disappear. They instead will remain hidden inside us, erupting at the slightest provocation with a venom we never knew we possessed. The woman who blurted out that she wished her husband were dead was stunned by her own remark. Who was that person who had spoken those words? Certainly not her.

No matter who it was that did the leaving, the end of the marriage produces in each spouse intense anger and resentment toward the other. If we acknowledge these feelings as part of ourselves and recognize their source, we can ventilate them and let them play themselves out so that eventually they will no longer bind up our thoughts and energies to no purpose. In the first stages of divorce they can act as the fuel we need to pull apart from the old relationship, if we will let them. They can keep us from building up momentary surges of nostalgia for the past into a binding fantasy of an ideal marriage which may never have existed in fact, but which can now prevent us from ever being free to live in the present.

Accept these feelings as emotional truth, even if they do not seem to fit the external facts. Recognize that your anger is real, that part of you resents your former spouse for no longer being there, for "creating" the misery of your single state—even if you were the one who left the marriage. If denied or suppressed, anger will emerge in more devious and destructive ways. You may project it on the behavior of your ex-spouse, hiding it in the rationalization of "I'm not angry, it's just that he's being so impossible over the property settlement." This way lies the continuation of battles from your past marriage. Anger often is internalized as a physical ailment of some kind—as Helen's stomachache could well be—which becomes a physical manifestation both of an emotional reaction that cannot be accepted in any other form, and a painful punishment for experiencing the reaction in the first place. Perhaps the most common effect of anger denied is depression, a kind of paralyzing standoff between powerful negative feelings and an equally strong need to deny that they exist. So much emotional energy is required to keep the anger suppressed that there is little left over for any other activity.

When we recognize the real feelings behind the sudden emotion spillovers common to many people in the first months of divorce or separation, we learn a great deal about ourselves which we can put to productive use. Coming to this awareness often means breaking through lifetimes of conditioning by a culture which parcels out emotions according to sex. Women are supposed to be tender, emotional, pliant, patient, understanding, weak. They are to serve, nurture, bridge gaps, smooth over. They do not make waves, they get along. Men are silent, unemotional, strong, aggressive. Women cry, men stifle their sobs. Women cling, men stand straight. The price we pay for accepting these assumptions is the denial of the full range of internal resources we all possess, men and women. A woman no more "owns" tenderness than a man "owns" aggressiveness. A woman who recognizes the validity of her anger can use it to move toward self-assertion and security as a single person. A man who can cry without shame in acceptance of honest feelings of grief over his lost marriage can more quickly move beyond this grief to a more satisfying new life. Without this recognition, such feelings will become more powerful and will keep the past alive as the major influence on the present and future.

"I GET THE STRONG IMPRESSION
I'M SOME KIND OF PARIAH"

Helen's interpretation of her friends' behavior, while not entirely inaccurate, is strongly colored by her own negative attitude toward herself. At this stage in her separation she is obsessed with finding an answer to why it happened, what she did wrong. Like others in her situation, she stays up late sifting and resifting through events of the past, trying to pick out the clues to just what went wrong. Was it me? Should I have sensed sooner that something was amiss and tried to correct it? Or was it all his fault?

The impulse to evaluate the lost marriage is typical of the recently separated or divorced; their attempts to examine their relationship objectively can be a first step toward increased self-awareness and also a healthy exercise of problem-solving abilities. However, as with Helen, most people are still so emotionally bound up in the marriage that objectivity rapidly turns into either self-justification or self-punishment. They think of it in terms of a courtroom trial, and in their emotional need to arrive at a verdict, end up playing all the parts themselves—judge, jury, victim, defendant, witness. No matter the effort to see justice triumph, the trial is almost always rigged: years of marriage have locked both partners into the familiar roles of blamer and martyr, long-sufferer and instigator, the breaker and the mopper-up.

Such postmarital evaluations keep the old blame-making machinery running because they seek answers to the wrong question. "Who did it?" can result in only one of two answers—both equally wrong—"me" or "my mate." There are some early indications in Helen's story ("considering the mess I've made of my life") that, when the evidence is in, she may blame herself for the dissolution of her marriage. If she chooses this path, it could well represent a pattern of behavior that had been ingrained during the years of life with her husband and even before: I am inadequate, nothing I can do is good enough, when something goes wrong I am guilty. The opposite approach—it's all his/her fault, it never would have happened if it hadn't been for his/her nagging, irresponsibility, egotism, running around—is equally corrosive to the self-esteem of both partners and to the speed with which the marriage can be legally and emotionally terminated.

If Helen can keep her energies focused on "what went wrong in the marriage?" and not "who did it?" she is more likely to find an answer close to the truth than if she falls into the trap of assigning guilt, placing blame, and wreaking vengeance. Admittedly the temptation to seek out heroes and villains is strong; there are occasions when we would like to assign white hats and black hats to people around us. If we are honest with ourselves, though, sooner or later we will stop trying to impose black-and-white judgments on facts which are not so simple.

Yet, society practically forces divorced people to define their experience in terms of blame, failure, and guilt. Almost all of us were brought up believing in marriage as the ultimate goal, the final problem-solver, the preordained institution in which we would live out our lives, each partner being everything to the other. Society sees to it that we pay the price for having denied the truth of this ideal picture. Divorce courts, forcing both parties into a system associated with criminals and law-breakers, reinforce the notion that one party is innocent and the other guilty. Although the adoption by some states of "no-fault" divorces has taken the element of blame out of financial settlements, it has not removed it from the divorce proceedings. Blame has simply been shifted to the area of child custody and visitation rights. What often happens as a result of this shift in battlegrounds is that the husband and wife, frustrated by law from seeking revenge through economic means, take out hostilities through their children—who are the ultimate casualties of bitter custody fights.

You can make your divorce an opportunity for personal growth if you channel the healthy impulse to assess your past marriage away from the issue of guilt and blame and toward questions that will yield answers you can put to productive use in your new life: What kind of person have I (and my former mate) become that made the marriage unsatisfactory? What were the real needs—of myself and my former mate—that the marriage met? Which of these needs were based on unrealistic expectations of what marriage is supposed to provide? What are the alternatives I can accept to the socially approved idea that my mate is nothing more than an extension of myself? How can I recognize the difference between an adult relationship of shared feelings and a union in which the needs of one partner are satisfied only at the expense of the other partner?

These are not easy questions; the answers will not be immediately forthcoming, nor do they lie only in your marital history. However, what they can tell you about yourself and your requirements for a marital relationship can make the next one (if you want a next one) better.

"IT'S GETTING SO THAT I PREFER MY OWN SOLITUDE. . . ."

Helen's concern over the reaction of her friends and her own wish to withdraw from them is typical of many men and women in the first months of single life, who are so convinced of their own worthlessness and so afraid of facing the world without their spouse that they retreat into a shell. Like Helen, they interpret changes in attitude on the part of acquaintances as extensions of their own self-chastisement, and are puzzled when once-close friendships seem not so rewarding or supportive as before. They are so wrapped up in their own problems that they fail to recognize a critical fact: their friends are reacting in terms of their own emotional needs and conflicts which the divorce itself has set off, not in response to any judgments as to the guilt or innocence of the divorced person. Helen's fear that the incident in the supermarket is part of a pattern is not entirely unfounded, although it is not the kind of social ostracism she fears. Although we cannot know exactly what was going through the other woman's head when she ducked behind the display of gardening equipment, it probably included a mixture of several conflicting feelings which Helen stirred up—not Helen as Helen, but Helen as separated woman. First, the simple confusion of what to say. Would it seem cold and unfeeling not to mention Helen's separation, or would bringing it up be too painful for Helen's fragile state? Rather than say anything, she found it easier to sidestep the problem and simply avoid Helen.

At a less conscious level, Helen may have triggered some feelings in the other woman which neither she nor Helen is aware of. Quite unwittingly, Helen by her very presence has aroused dissatisfactions within this woman concerning her own life and marriage which she would prefer to ignore. A divorce of a close friend or relative unconsciously causes us to reflect on our own marriages. If the woman in the supermarket is at all typical, she has had moments when she wondered whether she had married the right man, whether her life would be different if she were not married, whether she is as happy as she could be. The fact that she is still married reveals her decision—that in spite of all the problems, married life is better than anything else, and she will live with it. The sight of Helen will reactivate these thoughts; if she is more than a little ambivalent toward her own marriage, these thoughts may be too unpleasant and self-incriminating for her to accept. And so she avoids Helen, and though the avoidance is her problem, not Helen's, Helen can see only that she is "some kind of pariah."

A further complicating factor in such circumstances, one over which Helen has no control, stems from fantasized behavior which the other woman could be projecting on Helen. Let's say this woman has indulged in moments of reverie in which she is single again and can live the life of the carefree, seductive, sought-after woman which marriage had denied her. If these fantasies are vivid, Helen stands no chance of convincing her that the reality of divorce is something quite different. In her fantasies this woman knows how *she* would behave, and she unconsciously transfers the image of the "gay divorcee" she would like to be onto Helen. These fantasies are more likely to flare up in social situations where husbands are present than in the supermarket. And they are not always fantasies. Many men will assume that a divorced woman is looking for some sexual solace, and many divorced women do try to latch on to other husbands to replace the one they lost. Usually, however, the kind of social reaction which convinces many divorced women that they have a big scarlet "D" on their foreheads is fueled more by fantasy than by fact.

The task before Helen is not to become an instant expert on the psychological health of her friends. What she must realize, for her own well-being, is that changes in their reactions toward her spring from their own feelings that she, as a divorced woman, has set off. She can do nothing about these feelings; they are the concern of her friends, not of hers. Until she accepts the fact that it is *them,* not *her,* she will continue to interpret every real or imagined social slight as further proof of her own guilt and worthlessness.

More perplexing to Helen was her own cool reaction to her next-door neighbor, a woman Helen could see was doing her best to offer moral support. In this case it was Helen herself who withdrew, who found the frequent get-togethers over morning coffee less fulfilling than they had been. She was, in fact, increasingly depressed at every meeting, and was beginning to fear that her separation had destroyed the chance for her to have any close friends.

What Helen is experiencing is common to many women as well as men in her situation, and at this stage is not necessarily destructive. Her feeling of increasing distance from people she has known, if not carried to extremes, is in fact a healthy sign that she is recognizing the reality of her single state and is moving toward a new life. Her withdrawal from these friends frees her to move toward new relationships more suited to living singly. Just because Helen feels less comfortable with—or comforted by—her next-door neighbor does not guarantee that she will feel this way in every new relationship. Practically speaking, Helen and her neighbor no longer have quite so much in common as they did when Helen was married. If Helen hasn't found it out already, she will discover when she gets a job and begins to form a social life as a single woman that many of the common interests which made friendship with her neighbor rewarding in the past will begin to disappear. Her neighbor will continue to talk about herself as half of a couple, about what *we* did, or where *we* are going, and Helen will feel left out in the cold. By the same token, Helen will be savoring new experiences as a single woman which her neighbor will not be able to share. This does not mean Helen should never see her neighbor again, or that they won't remain friends—only that she should not blame herself or her neighbor if they no longer enjoy the same kind of friendship in the future.

It is only natural during the initial months of separation for Helen to cling to old friendships, and even seek from them greater emotional support than they provided in the past. In her abandonment, she needs expressions of understanding and sympathy to convince herself that she is still a person worth liking. At the same time, she should understand that the same friends who offer consolation also offer the unpleasant reminder that she is divorced while they are still married, and that this discrepancy may make her feel uncomfortable around them. If she continues to lean heavily on their support, or to think that she will be disappointed by everyone she meets, she will remain stuck in the habits of her past marriage and never make new friends. Like the man out of work who continues to set up lunch dates to talk about what is going on in the old office with his colleagues who are still on the job, she will find herself clinging to social relationships no longer relevant to the facts of her new life.

The first months of separation or divorce provide the time for sorting out long-standing friendships. We should examine them carefully and not be afraid that by moving away from those which are no longer mutually rewarding we are being antisocial and selfish, or are doomed to remain friendless forever. Upon examination, some of these relationships will turn out to have been only friendships of function—convenient compatibilities between couples, not between persons, involving baby-sitting and child-watching, company while shopping, acceptable adjuncts at a dinner party or a bridge game. Since our lives have changed, we should expect these friendships to change as well. Other friends may be friends of routine, maintained more out of habit than desire. When we alter our routine by becoming single, these friendships often fall by the wayside, often without our even noticing that they have died.

This period also offers the opportunity to reach out to new people with interests more compatible with our own, or to deepen relationships with men and women who had only been casual acquaintances before. In my own case, I became close friends with one of my colleagues at work. Until my separation, we had never progressed much farther than "Hello, how've you been doing?" but when I responded one day to his expression of concern over my apparent misery, we began what has turned out to be an extremely rewarding friendship for us both.

The healing process of mourning, as highlighted in Helen's story, can now be summarized: In our emotions divorce produces a *separation shock* which can equal in intensity the feelings evoked by the actual death of a husband or wife; and it sets in motion reactions similar to those which an actual death can cause: initial denial that the relationship has ended, producing at first a retreat into a fantasy life where it can still live on; powerful feelings of hostility and anger toward the absent person for having abandoned us to an intolerable life without him or her; pervasive feelings of guilt, internalized or projected, over things we did and didn't do during the relationship; a withdrawal from those parts of our past too painful to cope with (or too irrelevant to survive in our present lives); a gradual testing and retesting of reality; and an eventual letting-go from the influence of the past relationship so that a new life can begin.

For purposes of clarification this process of necessity has been oversimplified; obviously we do not pass through these stages the way we go through high school, a grade at a time. The elements of mourning are inherent in each divorce, but the mixture and intensity of the stages vary widely, since no two individuals are the same. We bring to our divorce experience the sum total of our strengths and weaknesses as human beings, along with the unique world view our past history has given to us. Helen has not yet lived through this process; feelings of denial and anger still dominate much of her life. Yet even in her story we can see the healing taking place. The more she acts on the realities of her new life as an independent person, the more she internalizes these independent acts, the sooner she will be living in the present. Helen's story, while unique to her, nevertheless springs from the wide range of possible emotional responses common to us all which a divorce or separation can summon forth.

WHEN IS
ENOUGH ENOUGH?

Because each of us is unique, it is impossible to make any flat statement about how long the process of mourning should take. My experience with divorced people suggests that mourning usually reaches its peak within the first six months of separation, and diminishes markedly thereafter—but this will vary widely. The most significant sign that you are coming out of mourning is the gut feeling that *you have survived,* that you can make it on your own, and that in spite of surges of nostalgia or resentment the past no longer completely dominates the present for you.

Also, many divorced people begin the mourning process before they separate. Many men and women have spent from six months to three years prior to their separation fully aware that their marriage was going to end, but for a variety of emotional, economic, or legal reasons were unable to break apart. They may have openly discussed the possibility of divorce with their spouses, or may have continued to rage and fight—but in many instances were already beginning the painful emotional process of pulling apart. When a woman in one of my seminars realized six months before her separation that the marriage was over, she began taking out books on divorce from the library, "I snuck in and out of that place as if I were a criminal," she confessed. "First I would check to see if anyone was there that I knew, then I would grab the books, rush through the check-out desk, and hide them in a big bag. In case a friend saw me I had a big story prepared about how I was getting the books for someone who was taking a course. I hoped that the librarian thought I was a teacher or social worker or something. When I got home I read them as fast as I could and took them right back."

If, at least to some extent, you accepted the end of your marriage months or even years before it actually terminated, you may well have felt an immediate surge of relief once the decision was made, as if a noose had loosened from your neck. As a result, you may be able to go through the mourning process more quickly after the break-up itself than men and women for whom a divorce comes as a partial or total surprise. Or, if you never really engaged your emotions in your marital relationship but always remained somehow aloof from real closeness with your mate, chances are that the divorce will not cut any lifelines, since there were none to start with.

Whatever the variations in schedule or impact of mourning, the positive benefits are greatest and most lasting when you recognize and accept, rather than resist, your feelings. These can include anger, fear, anxiety, resentment, vulnerability, and guilt—side by side with equally strong urges to return to the past. Your feelings may have always been bottled up inside you; now is the time to let them out and make positive use of them.

Some people never emerge from the mourning period. These are the women who say after ten years of being divorced, "Yes, I want to fall in love again, but I'm not ready yet." Or the man who continues to vilify his former wife for his present misery years after his marriage ended.

How can we tell when the mourning process is ended? When:

- resentment and bitterness towards your former mate have subsided from twenty-four-hour obsessions to occasional flashes of anger
- you spend less time complaining about problems and more time trying to solve them.
- you begin calling up old friends and making new

friends, in recognition of the fact that you have nothing to be ashamed of.

- you begin making decisions based on your interests and pleasure—taking a course, attending a play, entertaining friends.
- the opposite sex is no longer stereotyped as threatening or despicable, and statements lumping all men or women together no longer seem accurate to you.
- you realize that you are not the only person ever to have been divorced, that other normal people have had the courage to end an unhappy marriage.
- you come to accept divorce as the only possible solution to a self-destructive marriage, and not a punishment for having failed.

A woman who was trying to explain how one knows when the worst is over summarized it this way: "You lift up, kind of."

CHAPTER 4

Beyond Adjustment: Avoiding the Nine Emotional Traps of the Past

CESSATION OF PAIN IS NOT THE WHOLE STORY

In even the most difficult of divorces, the pain of parting eventually subsides, and then ceases. Lessons are learned, conclusions drawn, bargains struck, and, in time, life somehow becomes manageable once again. What we make of this life will depend on how well we have understood the process of mourning we have lived through, and how firmly we have grasped the meaning of those unfamiliar and powerful feelings which boiled to the surface during that period. Whether we settle for a life which is merely livable or elect to follow the riskier but much more rewarding path of personal growth will be determined by how we use these feelings to discern our real needs and marshal our efforts to fulfill them. The choice we make can mean the difference between sitting home in a warm bath of self-pity or using time for pleasure and growth.

The divorce crisis provides an excellent learning situation—a time when we are forced to try our new ways of acting, thinking, and feeling as single people. A divorce becomes creative in the degree to which we internalize these tentative departures from our married selves—the seeds beneath the snow—and come to accept them as the preeminent definers of who we are. Because I know from personal and professional experience how rewarding this process can be, I am concerned by the number of people who get stuck midway in the process of going from "spouse" through "spouse no longer" to "independent person." Having emerged from the mourning process intact, they strike a bargain with life: in exchange for the cessation of pain they agree not to ask for any exhilarating pleasure. In the first months of their divorce the pain was so great that this bargain seemed more than fair. "Don't rock my boat," they say. "It's taken me all this time to adjust to my divorce. I've learned to expect less from life, because I can't stand being disappointed again. Isn't that enough?"

And yet, as the months and years pass by, they find that an anesthetized existence isn't enough. Yes, they enjoy many pleasures: they read, they attend cultural events, they see other people, they find solace in their work—but still the question remains in the backs of their minds: "Is this all there is? Am I to be a permanent spectator at the game of life?" I have only the greatest respect for men and women who have lived through a painful divorce and arrived at a point where they feel emotionally stable and relatively free from pain. I have met many such people in my seminars-some of them divorced for as many as ten years—whose lives have become orderly again and who believe in all sincerity that they have made the most of a bad situation. And yet that nagging question has brought them to my seminars in the hope of finding some alternative to the kinds of lives they are leading.

These people are torn between their basic dissatisfaction with themselves as they are and their fear of the changes that are likely to follow an admission of this dissatisfaction. Instead of seeking the kind of life they would really like, they use their energies to devise elaborate rationalizations which "prove" that they are as contented as circumstances will permit. Their fear of self-knowledge is so great that they deny themselves the chance to become the people they are capable of becoming. They settle for so much less than they could have, convincing themselves all the time that it is all they deserve or will ever get. However, what they *say* and what they really *feel* are miles apart; and behind their rationalizations is a seething discontent with their "adjustment."

THE NINE EMOTIONAL
TRAPS OF THE PAST

I will always be indebted to a woman in one of my early seminars whose experience so clearly illustrates the seductive appeal of turning a temporary refuge from pain into a permanent way of life. Let's call her Evelyn Hoffman. An intense woman in her mid-forties who had been divorced for a little over two years. Evelyn joined the group because she had just moved to town and wanted to meet some new people with interests and experiences similar to hers. As the weeks passed, it became evident that she was an outgoing person who was quickly finding a comfortable niche in her new community; certainly she was one of the most articulate and respected members of the seminar.

After the last session had ended, she asked if she could speak with me privately. "I thought you might be amused by something I found the other day when I was unpacking boxes," she began. "About a year ago my college alumni magazine asked me to write an article, and I decided to do something on my divorce. I had just gone through ten months of hell after my husband walked out on me, and had finally gotten to the point where I could face the world again. That was the worst period in my life. I was really proud of myself for having come through in one piece, and I thought other women would like to know it could be done. It's funny how people change, though. Last night when I read the article again, it was as if a different person had written it. She sounds sort of selfish to me now. I'm still proud of the way I survived, but if I were to write it today I wouldn't make it sound so final or so negative.

"That period was really more like an intermission than the end of the play. I suppose the emotional shock was so fresh that I needed to take a temporary leave of absence from life. But that's what it was, temporary. A necessary step to something more."

With Evelyn's permission, I have since used her article in my seminars to show the difference between remaining trapped in the past and moving into the present. Members of the seminars always express great respect for the tremendous strides she made since the break-up, yet they can also spot in her story at least some of the traps we all unwittingly stumble into which keep us from making the most of our new lives.

This is her article:

Here we are, divorced women with the courage to stand firm against the pseudo-sophistication of life today. We've read the reviews, and we'll take the old days when life was simpler. Oh, we've made the cocktail party scene. Some of our old friends still ask us out, and we know we're supposed to "circulate," but then why is it that even the most innocent conversation with an old married friend (male) turns his wife into the green-eyed monster?

Okay, we should have realized that was a bad idea. We try one of those single get-togethers where nobody knows anyone else, but it's just what we knew it would be: a tacky banquet room in a second-rate restaurant, lots of nervous laughter and hyper-active sniffing around. In that atmosphere our natural friendliness gets ground into the rug. Things get off to a bad start when an over-hearty greeter pins a corny "Hello! My name is ————" tag on our dress. We picture a lifetime of bad drinks, paper cups, and awkward introductions stretching before us. And those people are all such losers, so dreary and apathetic! Fifteen minutes is enough to tell us that. Apparently all the witty and attractive men are already married, safe at home with their wives.

But so what? We see the empty years ahead (more than we care to dwell on, thanks to modern medicine) and yes, we fear a lonely old age, but we'd rather be alone than stuck again with another lemon. We've still got our pride; we know we're too good for that. Yes, we still want sexual fulfillment, but not for us the adolescent dating and the constant hassling with men out for a good time. We want something *forever* and profoundly *good* this time around.

We don't have to settle for anything less, so we go to the library and take out those long novels we've always wanted to read. We lay in a bottle or two of good sherry, relax, and let things come to us. We refuse to prowl around the edges of other people's lives.

In the meantime we don't let ourselves go to pot. We continue to exercise, eat sensibly, dress well. After all, *some* people still think we're attractive. We move away to a new town, find a job, start over. We're convinced we have something to offer. Maybe the job isn't everything we hoped it would be, but then we remember that businessmen these days are so busy making money and charging up the ladder of success that they don't have any time to show personal interest in their employees.

And then, while we are watching a television drama (why can't life be like that?) and finishing off a sweater for our brand-new grandchild, who should breeze in but our grown-up college sophomore, away for a few days from the groves of academe. Suddenly we know everything is all right. The parties, the dating, the disappointing job—they all vanish in the glow of living in a real home again, not just a furnished house. We are awash in well-being. We should have known it all along: this is where our real happiness lies.

Like members of my seminars—indeed, like Evelyn herself—you may have mixed emotions about this story. On the one hand, we can only admire the fact that she refuses to throw in the towel. She has come out of her divorce with dignity intact, she still keeps herself looking well, and she has made some efforts to meet new people. On the other hand you may have also detected a bitter and resigned tone, an undercurrent of dissatisfaction which belies her ultimate statement of happiness. You may feel, as Evelyn did later, that she was in fact assigning herself to emotional retirement when part of her still wanted to live. If so, you have probably identified some of the following traps of the past she has fallen into:

Trap #1: *Unwarranted generalizations.* We all unwittingly adopt generalizations which keep us from acting in our own best interests. This habit is especially prevalent among divorced men and women who, while insisting that their own experiences are unique, nevertheless continue to act according to inhibiting generalities about themselves and other people. In this case Evelyn—by assuming that all divorced women feel as she does ("we," divorced women)—is laying the groundwork to explain personal defeat right off the bat. If her plight is so pervasive, what can she as one individual be expected to do about it? So long as she believes that her attitude is universal, she will feel justified in maintaining it. Unexamined beliefs about the opposite sex serve the same purpose. Statements like "no man can be trusted" or "all women are possessive" reveal more about the speaker's attitude than they do about men and women in general. What people who make these statements are really saying is, "I have a good reason for not seeking out new relations with men (or women). It is they who are flawed; only I am flawless." Many men and women will profess ignorance as to why their best efforts to find someone new always come to naught, and yet when pressed will admit to a belief along the lines of "men are only after one thing" or "all women are tramps." It is unwarranted generalizations such as these, often based on one or two bad experiences, which keep the divorced person from ever taking the chance of being pleasantly surprised by being proved wrong.

Trap #2: *The self-fulfilling prophecy.* Like generalizations, preconceptions can serve as protective shields against trying out new behavior or attitudes (frightening because of their very newness), even when the new ways may be in our best interests. Because the writer knew in advance what the singles party would be like, she found only what she was looking for. Maybe it *was* dreary; parties often are. Maybe the people *were* losers, but fifteen minutes wasn't much time to find out for sure.

Although Evelyn's experience at the cocktail party may well reflect society's attitude toward the divorced woman (rather than any predatory plans of her own), I think it is fair to assume that she went to the singles party to meet new people, and especially new men. There is obviously nothing wrong in doing that. However, once she got to the party her fear of a new relationship took over. "Closeness with a man, or anything leading to closeness, is dangerous," she hears her fear telling her. "Remember how your ex-husband hurt you. Don't risk it again." Consequently she backs off from even casual small talk, rationalizing that all the people there are on the prowl. They have become, to her, generalized extensions of her own fear rather than real people in their own right. She can find out what they are really like (including the possibility that they are losers or on the make) only by talking to them. This is precisely what she avoids doing. She has thus unwittingly fallen into a perfect distancing device to keep her from taking even the first step toward meeting someone new. Her fear has won out over the motivation which brought her out of the house in the first place. Her memories of hurt from her past marital break-up are too strong to let her take the chance. (Given her fear of closeness, I would also question whether in fact she was projecting the friendliness she claimed. More than likely she was unconsciously sending out "stay away, you evil men" signals, signals that she will transmit in *any* new social situation where men are present.)

Distancing devices can be self-preserving in the initial stages of divorce. But when carried past the first months, they keep us from ever reaching out to another person, and can thus destroy any chances for future happiness.

Trap #3: *Unreal expectations.* As Evelyn was to realize later, throughout the article she betrays a range of unreal expectations about what life should offer. This is a common trap divorced men and women fall into to justify their miserable state. Having high standards sounds like a good excuse for not attempting a difficult challenge. This is the attitude behind statements like, "If it can't be perfect, I don't want any part of it." Because reality never manages to live up to Evelyn's expectations, she opts out. Take her attitude toward sex. Of course we all want what she wants, a forever and profoundly good relationship. But what chance is she giving herself? Very little. Such a relationship cannot be certified in advance, any more than love can be guaranteed to last forever. As long as she clings to the knight-in-shining-armor image, she will always be disappointed in anything else. Rather than face her needs openly, she "solves" her conflict by setting impossibly high standards and waiting for things to happen to her. She believes that if she doesn't meet the man of her dreams (and it's difficult to see how she could) it won't be her fault. So with the best of intentions, she has unconsciously shut herself off from that which she wants most to achieve. This is not to say that she must hit every bar and party in town—or that she has got to find a man if she is ever to be happy again; only that her expectations for meeting a man are not very realistic, and that when she has reached the point at which she is ready for a new relationship they could then become a serious obstacle—and one of her own making.

The writer is also disappointed in her job because it isn't everything she hoped it would be—but here, too, she perhaps has unreal expectations of the kinds of needs work can fulfill. Work can and should be rewarding in more than monetary terms alone. But work cannot encompass the full spectrum of emotional needs that a personal relationship can. The writer's statement that today's businessman is self-centered and thoughtless (another generalization!) could well reflect inappropriate personal needs (a boss interested in taking her out?) she half-consciously had hoped her job would fulfill. When she expects her work to take the place of a personal life, she is once again guaranteeing disappointment.

Trap #4: *Disasterizing*. Space scientists work on the assumption that if something can go wrong, it will. Translating a precept of applied research into everyday life has its perils. It is one thing to plan realistically for contingencies and another to act on the belief that the worst will always happen. Evelyn here sees the empty years ahead as if she has already lived them. How does she know they will be empty? They can be, but only if she makes them so, and as she was later to find out, they are not proving to be empty after all. Disasterizing means always being on the defensive, flinching before you are hit, recognizing only fortune's slings and arrows. People who disasterize need every piece of bad news they can lay their hands on in order to justify their passive acceptance of an unsatisfactory life. Any sign of success gets turned around into an omen of future failure. One man in my seminar was terrified when he got a good grade on a paper in an evening course in law. "My God," he said, "Now the professor will think

I'm an expert, and he'll be gunning for me at the final exam."

Trap #5:*Wallowing.* Disasterizing plays beautifully into wallowing. If life is really as bad as you think it is, aren't you within your rights to feel sorry for yourself? The writer of this article has set herself up for some pretty elegant wallowing: sherry, good novels, a cozy fire, the solace of a TV drama. Delightful in moderation, yes, but dangerous in excess. The more time she spends in these pastimes, the more they become excuses to avoid meeting new people and getting out of her rut. The more energy she puts into wallowing, the less she will have to build a life she won't want to escape *from* or feel sorry *for*.

The distinction between self-defeating wallowing and the necessary period of withdrawal during the mourning process is often hard to make. What is self-preservation at the outset of a separation can easily turn into a trap. You are probably wallowing if, after a year or more since your divorce, you are still clinging to reasons to feel sorry for yourself, and using them as excuses to avoid taking necessary risks.

Trap #6: *Blame-making.* Because many divorced people are so disatisfied with themselves, they blame others for their problems instead of facing them squarely. Blame-making can sink even the sunniest personality in a sea of sourness, pessimism, and angry depression. In this article Evelyn, finds herself in just such a state. It's not me, she says, it's them. The men at the singles parties are losers and schemers, the host is overhearty, her boss (one assumes that when she says "businessman" she means her boss) is selfish. She is attributing to others qualities which she perhaps senses in herself, but which are too unpleasant to be accepted fully as hers. Because she is probably still clinging to her identity as wife, she unconsciously puts herself down as a loser, and labels her single-person social life as adolescent. Rather than face up to her own unease with herself, she finds it easier to pass judgment, criticize, and belittle others. Instead, she should be asking herself, "Now that I am single, what have I learned from my past marriage *about myself* and *what can I do now* to make my life more satisfying?"

Trap #7: *Flight from oneself.* Closely related to Trap #6, this trap assumes that since the causes of one's problems are external, then the solution must be to move away, get a new job, start over somewhere else. If understood properly, getting a fresh start can be a therapeutic step. One woman told me she postponed leaving her husband until she had gotten a job as manager of a ski resort three hundred miles way. "I didn't even let my married children know where I was at first," she said. "I had no telephone, either. I needed that time to do some thinking in a totally new environment with a completely different set of people. It was really a good thing for me to do. I got my own feelings pretty well sorted out in my mind and I also learned that a lot of other people there had problems much more serious than mine."

However, if people move to a new community in the belief that they can leave their fears and anxieties behind, they will be disappointed. Evelyn made a move to a new town; when she wrote the article she had hoped that by starting over she could erase her unhappy past. But as she later learned, the move was just the beginning, not the entire solution. Flight from oneself need not involve a physical move, of course. Compulsive workers, eaters, watchers of television, alcoholics—these are all people who seek escape from their problems.

Trap #8: *Living through others.* This is perhaps the cruelest trap of all, especially for women who have been brainwashed from birth to believe that their personal fulfillment lies solely in their family. Finding themselves suddenly single, they often clutch frantically at any vestiges of their former lives which once gave them happiness. As with Evelyn, children often become the vehicle by which they seek to continue their old identities. A creative divorce can bring about closer and more rewarding relationships with our children but, paradoxically, the very joys that our children provide can also keep us mired in the past—if they are our *only* joys. The eagerness with which Evelyn seized on the visit of her college-age child to justify her life is poignant proof that she is still seeking fulfillment in past roles, not in present possibilities. She still persists in thinking of herself primarily as a homemaker and mother, even though her children no longer live with her and are developing lives of their own. She need not abandon the joys of motherhood (or grandmotherhood) to live in the present, but she should guard against their becoming her only reason for living. We cannot help but be disappointed when we live only through others; and continuing disappointment can turn into bitterness.

Trap #9: *Yearnings of the half-person.* The unspoken and unacknowledged plea of this article is, "I need someone to make me a whole person again." In spite of all her distancing devices and rationalizations, the writer still feels that only when she has found another husband can she be happy again. Instead of taking the opportunity to develop her own strengths as an independent person, she has directed (and then thwarted) her efforts toward finding Mr. Right, the man who can complete her image of herself by reinstating her in the position of wife. Evelyn claims she has come to terms with her life as a divorced woman, but in fact she still thinks of herself as only one half a person, incomplete without a husband.

As Evelyn herself later said, "Thank God I didn't remarry then. I was so mixed up and defensive that I probably would have ended up with a second husband just like my first. It's really only been in the last six months that I've begun to learn something about the kind of person I've become, and the kind of relationship I know I need. And I don't need marriage the same way I did when I married for the first time. I'm a lot more independent now, and I've got more things going for me."

THE MAN'S
EXPERIENCE

I am grateful to Evelyn for having written that article when she did, because so many of the men and women in my seminars arrive at that kind of life and think that it is the end, instead of the beginning. Men, too, run the same danger of escaping into the past. Men are just as emotionally devastated by divorce as women. They feel the same impact; they bleed equally. And just as many men as women sleepwalk their way through a divorce right into a "new" life which repeats their unhappy past in every important respect. The strength of the impact of divorce on men is a fact most women (and many men) find very hard to accept. They can be much more frightened than women by feelings of vulnerability, helplessness, loneliness, and fear that erupt within them during the crisis of divorce—frightened, and horrified that their reactions should be so "womanly." Women can seek help from friends, books, magazines, professional counseling. Men are not supposed to need any help. As a result, men have developed even greater capacities than women for running away from their feelings and avoiding the opportunities for personal growth that a creative divorce offers.

At the outset of a divorce or separation, this may not appear to be true. Usually it is the wife who seems totally destroyed, while the husband, to all external appearances, sails on smoothly. After all, a man still has his job to tell him who he is. His identity has always included the roles of husband and father, but its largest component has been the image of independent, self-sufficient wage-earner. Often he has hobbies—golf, fishing, hunting—which reinforce his strong-man facade. A woman, on the other hand, has usually put all her emotional eggs in the marriage basket and when the bottom drops out she feels her identity has been completely shattered. The importance of marriage, still, to the feminine identity is revealed by the woman who is telling a new friend about her three children: "Well, my older boy is a mining engineer, the younger works for the city, and my daughter is married to an advertising executive."

Furthermore, society accords men greater freedom to go out, meet new people, do things. Ex-husbands do not generally have to worry about baby-sitters, nor do they have to fear what the neighbors will say. The point needs little elaboration here: it is a fact of American life that members of the opposite sex are more available to men than to women and simply more plentiful. No one gives a second thought to a fifty-year-old man in the company of a woman fifteen or twenty years his junior, but if the ages were reversed, eyebrows would rise to the hairline. Society is becoming more tolerant toward women who actively seek out men (including younger men) but changing social mores is a slow process.

Ironically, these advantages which men enjoy over women can prevent them from ever moving into the present. Because in the initial stages of separation they find it so much easier than women to escape from their problems—into work, or a hobby, or a frantic social life—they can successfully sidestep the painful confrontation with their own feelings which is a necessary part of coming to terms with the past. What may have started out as a normal initial reaction to the divorce crisis turns into a perpetual way of life. It is Trap #7, Flight from one-self. These are the men who work sixteen-hour days, seven days a week, who years after their divorce will say, "I sure wish I had the time to meet some interesting women." Work is all-consuming but not all-satisfying, yet they are afraid to chance any alternative way of life which might be more rewarding.

For a man, flight can also take the form of the eternal night on the town. His apartment is just a place to change clothes; every evening sees him with another woman, at another bar, going to another party. He wears the latest styles, has the most modish haircut, takes the most frequent vacations. He is the gay blade par excellence. Many women view this flight with envy, and turn a deaf ear to the notion that it is almost always self-defeating. What's so bad about it?" they say. "I wish I could get out of the house every night."

There is nothing "bad" about such behavior during the first months of a separation or divorce. It can be part of the way in which a man (or, of course, a woman) polishes up rusty single-person skills. When carried to excess, however, bachelorizing becomes a means to avoid acknowledging real feelings and a trap which keeps a man from living in the present. Furthermore, locker-room bragging notwithstanding, most men soon find this way of life monumentally boring. They want something more, but fear the risks they must take to get it.

The comparative ease with which men can run away from their feelings explains in large part a difference in recovery rates I have observed between divorced men and women. Women, with a greater part of their total identity destroyed during a divorce, often hit rock bottom during the first months of separation. For them, coming to grips with their emotions and seeking out a workable new way of life is a simple matter of survival. They have little choice. Men, on the other hand, have other roles to sustain them, and so may be able to suppress the sense that they are no longer complete persons.

What usually happens in these circumstances is that the woman, out of total immersion in the mourning process, will emerge a stronger, more secure person than the man, who never was able either to accept the enormity of his loss nor learn from it. If, after a year and a half or two, you were to plot their rates of growth on the same chart, the woman's would proceed from an initial low in the lower-left-hand corner to a high point in the upper-right-hand quadrant, while the man's would appear as a relatively horizontal line—neither as initially low nor as ultimately high as the woman's.

Men often play out their "I need a woman to complete me" needs in bed, sometimes with their ex-wives. Al, 41, couldn't seem to break off sexual relations with his former wife, even though they had been separated six months. "I don't know what the hell I'm doing," he told the group. "The actual sex is pretty good; it always was. But I feel lousy afterward. I know that there is so much wrong with our marriage. Muriel and I really have nothing in common any more except this. If I go back to her it will be the same nag, nag, nag. 'Why don't you make more money like so-and-so?' I can't take that crap any longer. But I still feel the old need, and when I do I don't want to pick up someone in a bar, so back I go to Muriel and the comfort she can give me. It's not only sex; we have a fourteen-year history together. But when I leave I always feel tense and irritable. She even asked me to move back in with her. I said I'll think about it, but I know I won't do it. And yet, the next time I see her I bet we'll jump in the sack."

The other emotional traps of the past ensnare just as many men as women. Men, too, have a full repertoire of unrecognized behavior which keeps them from living in the present. The generalizations, the disasterizing, the unreal expectations—men fall victim to them all. Women have no trouble spotting some in operation. They have probably spent more evenings than they care to think about listening to someone else's ex-husband complain about what a bitch his former wife was, how she "took" him for every dime he had, how the divorce was all her fault. They may also have run across men like Al, looking for a woman to take care of them and "make them whole," if only through the magic of a home-cooked meal. These are the little boys many divorced and single women say they are always meeting.

Less obvious to women are the traps which men set for themselves through fear of being rejected by the opposite sex. A man's fear of being turned down by a woman is something women often minimize. To a woman, constrained by custom to sit demurely at the edge of life's dance floor until a man comes and sweeps her away, the masculine prerogative to initiate a meeting can seem like heady stuff indeed. What freedom! No need for the subterfuges, the waiting, the "feminine wiles" that her fear of appearing "aggressive" lead her into. To her, the man's social role seems so simple: all he has to do is ask.

On the other hand men, and especially divorced men, see the possibility of rejection as an ever-present threat in new social situations, and will go to considerable lengths to avoid that threat. A divorced man, just like a divorced woman, feels bruised and devaluated as a person attractive to the opposite sex. He, too, finds a single social life unfamiliar. What is a man his age doing "dating" again? He, too, will make friends with the farthest corner of the room at a party, clutching a drink and studiously avoiding the glances of any women he finds attractive. He, too, will remain in his shell rather than taking the risk of walking across the room to talk to a woman he finds attractive. A forty-one-year-old man put it this way: "It's the whole teen-age routine all over again—the nervousness, the sweaty palms, the worry about how you look. Christ, I thought I was past all that. Last week at a dance I was talking at the bar with some other men, and I saw a woman across the room who looked interesting—you know, just sort of nice. But did I ask her to dance? No, All I could think of was how far it was from here to there, and what if she turned me down? Then I would have to walk all the way back and everyone would know what had happened."

He might appear to be an apathetic bar-fly, but that apparent apathy is often just plain fear. My friend Don, a bartender who caters many private parties, is sure of it:

"At any kind of dance or cocktail lounge, I'll give you odds that if there are two unattached women present, one extremely attractive and the other less striking, the men will go for the second one every time. They're all sure the good-looker will turn them down."

THE CREATIVE
ALTERNATIVE

Everyone has his or her own idea of happiness. To me, one of the most exciting consequences of coming to terms with the past is the freedom to strive for your own particular brand of well-being. A complete change of life-style is not required. One of the greatest rewards of living creatively in the present (as against existing passively, responding only to others' wishes and demands) is the freedom to savor each moment for the pleasure it may provide, to appreciate accustomed pastimes for themselves once again instead of as poor substitutes for an empty life, and to explore and expand the dimensions of the independent person you are becoming.

Living creatively in the present means accepting yourself for what you are—not what you think you should be, or wish you were, or fear you are—but the sum total of your actions, thoughts, and feelings now, at this point in time. People living in the present can accept occasional failure and disappointment without feeling inadequate, and can enjoy success without the need to belittle or exaggerate. Their self-esteem is not wholly dependent on what other people think about them; and because they also acknowledge the rights of others to think and act for themselves, they are less likely to get their feelings hurt or feel taken advantage of.

Far from encouraging smugness or complacency, living in the present means accepting responsibility for controlling your own life. It means renouncing the security that tomorrow will, indeed must, be just like yesterday. It means accepting the uncertainty that comes with continued growth and change. A person living in the present is able to say, "Uncertainty is a fact of life I not only accept but enjoy because it means I can try to shape things to my liking. I have the resources to handle new situations as they arise. A completely static life is really no life at all."

People living in the present have the courage to ask, "What do *I* want out of life?" without feeling guilty. They affirm the legitimate needs of others, but they also know that they cannot expect others to live their lives for them. They grant the urge, and relish the rewards, of pursuing their own intellectual and emotional growth, and of developing their creative inclinations. They approach learning in and out of school with enthusiasm, and do not hesitate to change or bypass situations in their personal or professional lives which are needlessly destructive. They try, and try again. They are willing to put up with a certain amount of discouragement and frustration in order to achieve a goal, but because they hold realistic expectations for success they can keep from banging their heads against stone walls. Success for them does not depend on someone else's defeat; they feel no need to put others down. Their strong drives to be productive, creative, and useful spring from the need to exercise personal talents, and not from fears of dependency, inadequacy, or inferiority. They can therefore distinguish between childish egotism and mature self-interest, between overbearing aggressiveness and appropriate self-assertion.

By the same token, people living in the present acknowledge their interdependence with others. They accept functional dependence on others for food, clothing, and housing—as well as emotional dependence for love, approval, and attention. People living in the present find such necessary interdependence enjoyable, although when the chips are down they can survive emotionally on their own. They accept the need—for men as well as for women—to experience the passive aspects of being cared for, nurtured, attended to, and are able to respond without feeling unduly obligated or guilty.

They recognize that being fed or sheltered or financially supported inevitably carries overtones of emotional dependence stemming from childhood, but they avoid confusing childish needs with mature interdependencies. They do not require their husbands or wives to be surrogate fathers or mothers who must always be on the spot to give instant gratification to every wish and need. They have learned that adults satisfy the desire for love by giving care and attention as well as by receiving them.

Living in the present means understanding that personal growth is not achieved without constant striving and more than a few serious setbacks. People living in the present admit their particular kinks and quirks which prevent them from getting the most from every single moment in life, but do not turn these limitations into excuses for not trying. They realize that they will not always be happy or completely satisfied with the way things are going, but they also know that unless they do their best to direct their lives they run the risk of becoming permanently bitter, self-hating, negative and apathetic people.

In the challenge of moving from the crisis of divorce through the process of mourning and into the present, the feelings of anxiety, guilt, and anger that erupted with separation are important assets. They can provide the fuel we need to overcome our resistance to change, they can tell us when we are settling for an existence below our expectations and abilities, and they offer important clues to how we can make our lives more satisfying.

For these reasons, people going through a creative divorce will guard against turning a temporary adjustment into a permanent pattern of life in which the price paid for stability is the denial of further growth. Even while making whatever temporary compromises are necessary to minimize further hurt, they will continue to listen to these feelings in order to avoid turning a temporary anesthetic into a lifelong numbness.

They will accept a certain amount of anxiety as a healthy sign that they are growing. A significant change in our self-image cannot help but provoke anxious moments, because it requires us to leave behind those aspects of our identities which provided support and comfort in the past but which are now getting in the way of our present lives. Trying and unfamiliar ways of feeling, thinking, and acting will inevitably provoke a certain amount of anxiety until we become accustomed to our new selves. In a creative divorce, manageable anxiety produces the charge which keeps us "up" for the challenges of the present, and prevents us from retreating into a protective—and constricting—cocoon.

Guilt, faced squarely, is a useful tool in the construction of our new identities. Following any kind of divorce, creative or not, every step away from past roles and obligations as wives, husbands, and parents inevitably reactivates the guilt which society has so effectively imposed on the divorced man or woman. Rather than not taking these steps, however, a creative divorce encourages you to reexamine the sources of your guilty feelings. Often these feelings stem not from something you did, but beliefs about what you should have done or not done. Many people can eventually live with the fact that their divorce was right, the only solution to a destructive situation, yet their unexamined feelings of guilt remain strong enough to keep them from enjoying their new lives. In a creative divorce guilt is deflected from continual self-punishment toward a constructive reevaluation of moral and ethical standards inherited from the past which may no longer apply to contemporary life. Often, to our own detriment, we never have questioned the precepts we grew up with. Today, however, life is changing rapidly and standards which were appropriate in one era are being overhauled. Now is the time to compare your system of values against your own experience, and decide for yourself how relevant and helpful it is in your new life. Take a good look at your attitudes toward marriage, the family, and the proper way men and women should behave. Do you still buy them *in toto?* Or do you see the need for modifications? You may find that much of your guilt arises from values which, upon examination, no longer seem appropriate to your present situation. Freeing yourself from unwarranted guilt releases energies you will need to cope with the very real problems of your new life.

Anger is recognized in a creative divorce as a normal, in fact inevitable, consequence of a marital break-up. Used constructively it generates the energy needed to stand up for one's rights and correct unjust or harmful states of affairs. Anger, the fuel required for pulling apart from our past marriages, can continue to alert us to obstacles blocking our growth as independent people. Anger unrecognized takes many forms—sarcasm, apathy, depression, bitterness, hostility. In a creative divorce anger is accepted for what it is and becomes translated into *appropriate action.* By taking some step to act on your own interests, you are reducing the anger you feel over your apparent helplessness, and therefore can use constructively the energies you would otherwise have to employ in masking your anger.

If you find your anger directed destructively toward others, you can channel it to a constructive social use. A woman in one of my seminars used her anger to embark on a new career. "I realized that I was furious over the fact that everyone connected with my divorce—both lawyers, the judges, everyone but me—was a man. I started going to a few discussion groups for women, and they led me to the women's studies center at the university. Now I'm looking into paralegal jobs. They certainly could use more women in that field."

Coming to awareness of our feelings and the meanings they hold for us is of central importance if we are to make the most of our new lives as single people. If we do not recognize them or accept their meaning during the mourning process they can be so overpowering and terrible as to block the chance for personal growth which a creative divorce makes possible. Because these feelings then remain so painful, we will settle for a life—any life—in which they will recede enough to no longer endanger emotional stability. We may have accomplished our primary objective of stopping the pain, but in the process we have assigned ourselves to a less than satisfactory life which only an elaborate series of rationalizations can convince us is a happy one.

A creative divorce, by tapping the feelings that emerged during the mourning process, makes it possible to maintain the momentum for change generated during this period and use it to continue your drive toward independence. Life then becomes a series of choices, not inevitabilities, and you can set about the challenging and exciting task of dealing with the realities of your new life, free from the traps of the past. Meeting these challenges is what I call living creatively in the present and, as the subsequent chapters illustrate, is a far more rewarding prospect than living as if the present were a repetition of the unhappy past.

CHAPTER 5

Coping with New Realities

NEW BEGINNINGS: ROASTING PANS AND ESPRESSO MACHINES

It was the seminar's next-to-last meeting, postponed from the previous week because of the Easter holidays, and members were exchanging accounts of what they had done over the Easter weekend. There was a buoyance and excitement in the room which told me that these men and women were beginning to grasp the full meaning of their divorce experience and were putting their hard-earned knowledge to creative use in the present. This is the time when the seeds beneath the snow begin to flourish and bear fruit, when shared stories of renewed competency, power, and self-direction become more and more frequent.

"I bought a roasting pan," a woman in her fifties who had left her husband and thirty years in the suburbs and moved to an apartment in the city, "so that I could give a dinner party. It sounds funny now, but when I moved out ten months ago I took just the bare minimum of kitchen equipment. I couldn't imagine ever wanting to entertain again.

"For me that pan was a coming-out symbol. I had been avoiding my old friends for months. But last month I had my windows cleaned for the first time since I moved in.

What a difference! I hadn't realized how gloomy all that dirt made life seem. That's when I said to myself it's about time I stopped living like a mole. I suddenly remembered how much fun it used to be to entertain, and I decided to have a party."

She put a lot of planning into the occasion, she reported, and the results were well worth it. "It was a real effort to pick up the telephone after all those months. I kept thinking that no one would want to come, now that I was divorced. But all my friends—my old married friends—accepted! They all sounded so glad to hear from me. And everybody had a good time. I varied the guest list to include some new friends as well as couples I had known when I was married. I wanted to let my old friends know that I was okay—you know, alive and well and living in San Francisco.

"All my old friends told me how well I looked and how much happier I seemed," Ann reported, but the most gratifying reaction was their surprise, bordering on envy, at her new life. "They were fascinated at being able to look out my living room window and see slices of life in the building across the street. I guess I had forgotten how glamorous living in town can seem when you spend most of your time in the suburbs. Well, it may not be all that glamorous, but it *is* exciting, and their reaction confirmed for me the fact that I had done the right thing.

"They also made me realize how far I have come in the last ten months. All those questions they raised—parking problems, getting around by myself, feeling safe—no longer faze me. Compared to my sheltered suburban friends, I felt like a real pro. And I guess I am, in a way."

For Ann, this party crystallized a growing pleasure in her new style of life which had been evolving in the previous months, and encouraged her to plan another evening, this time for her new single friends. "And," she concluded, "I decided that night to accept a job offer I've been toying with. Starting next week, I'll be giving lectures on art at half a dozen retirement community centers around the city."

"It's funny you should mention a roasting pan," said Arthur, a stocky man of thirty-eight who had been divorced for a year. "I was drifting around town last Thursday, feeling sorry for myself because this was the first Easter since the divorce that I wouldn't spend with my family. I happened to pass one of those fancy imported gift shops, and it had an Italian espresso machine in the window. I said to myself, 'Why the hell not?' so I bought it. I've wanted one of those things for years, but my wife always said they were too expensive. Money wasn't really that tight—we could always afford little extravagances—but since *she* didn't want one, that was that.

"Well, it wasn't all that expensive, and it's fun besides. When I got it home I decided I should have a formal christening, so I invited some people down the hall to drop in Saturday evening. It turned into a great party. Sort of open-ended—people invited other people. All those months I had lived in that singles apartment building, but I hadn't really gotten to know many of the tenants. Turns out they're pretty interesting, most of them divorced. I'm going out next Saturday with a woman I met that evening."

He stopped to think a moment, and then continued, "You know, that night I began to accept the apartment on its own terms and decided to take advantage of the athletic and social activities it has. Like tennis. When I was married I was always too busy around the house to get to the courts; my wife always had a full weekend schedule of repairs and yard work for me."

As Arthur himself realized, the espresso machine was not so much an ego prop or a material substitute for a missing family life as it was a tangible sign that he was beginning to think, feel, and act like a single person again. Often these stirrings are so slight and gradual that we need some kind of outside symbol to know that they are taking place. Then, like Ann, we can look back and appreciate the difference between the miserable half-persons we were right after our separation and the confident, independent persons we are rapidly becoming. Another man in the group put it this way: "It's as if I were standing at the prow of a ship. All I could see was empty water ahead, and I really wasn't sure if I was moving forward. But then, when I looked back, I could see the ship's wake showing me where I had been and how much progress I had made. I know the ship hasn't reached port yet, but by God I've come a long way since those first weeks when I was sure I would never survive."

UNSUSPECTED INNER RESOURCES

We should savor these moments of accomplishment, no matter their source, and take some legitimate pride in what they are telling us about our abilities to handle the realities of our new lives. For these realities are indeed challenging: planning a new career, living on a different income, juggling domestic and professional responsibilities, managing children, and making time for a new social life—these are challenges calling for our very best efforts. Unless we grant ourselves time to take a few bows for step-by-step progress, we can wear out our energies on what seems to be a never-ending treadmill.

I am reminded of Dolores, a woman in her mid-thirties with two young children, divorced for little more than a year after a very early marriage. In the first months of her separation she was completely helpless. She said her husband had made every important decision for her, and now she felt inadequate to manage her new life. No matter how hard she tried, to hear her tell it, she could never get on top of things. She thought she was too poorly educated, too passive, and too insecure ever to be competent as a single woman. Life was a struggle, and she thought she was losing. And yet she told the group the following facts about her life since the separation: She had found a less expensive apartment for her and the children, and had supervised the move by herself, something she had never had to do during her married life. She decided to enroll for training as a medical technician and, when she was told she would need typing skills to enter the program, scared up a friend's typewriter and taught herself how to type. At the time of the seminar she was in the middle of her training and, when pressed, admitted that she was one of the better students. Every day she drove thirty-five miles to and from school. To squeeze enough money from her limited budget for baby-sitting fees, she had arranged a complicated schedule that required her to get up at six o'clock, dress her son for school, drop her preschool daughter at the baby-sitter's home, take her son to school, make daily arrangements for him to be cared for after school until she got home, spend all day at school herself, then drive back, pick up the children in the evening, return home—and carry out her accustomed duties of cooking, cleaning, and spending time with the children.

"Wow!" in the words of an older woman in the group. "If that isn't coping, I don't know what is. If you can handle all that, you're really something. I would never have the energy to maintain your schedule."

Dolores was at first dumbfounded, and then enormously pleased, at the group's reaction. Like too many divorced men and women, she was so terrified of the prospect of single life that she was overlooking what the other members of the group recognized as tremendous accomplishments. Having made at least two major decisions concerning her future—moving to a new apartment and becoming a medical technician—she then proceeded to act on these decisions. The move alone constituted a major upheaval; changing residences, under the best of circumstances, is logistically complicated and emotionally upsetting for even the most experienced person. On top of this she was embarking upon a new career in addition to her responsibilities as the mother of young children.

Dolores, in short, had changed her whole life: her marital status, her home, her career, her financial state, her daily habits, and her social activities—any one of which studies have found produce internal stress. In view of the fact that she had been married at an early age to a dominant husband who made all the decisions and kept her in a position of almost total dependence, Dolores might have been expected to collapse under the weight of her new responsibilities. That she did not buckle under is testimony to her own abilities, although she was not allowing herself to recognize them. She could have retreated into depression; she could have given up and gone on welfare; she could have wasted her energies in continued legal hostilities against her ex-husband. What she did, instead, was to draw up a plan for her new life and then set about carrying it out. Her goal was realistic, and she clearly was well on her way to attaining it, step by step, even while she remained convinced that she was inadequate.

If Dolores, and other divorced men and women, could but recognize the resources they can rely on, they would feel far more confident and pleased with the progress of their new lives. First is the ability of time itself to help us forget past pain and rekindle our interest in the future. Part of time's healing power is the human body's unrelenting drive toward physical and emotional health. As soon as a crisis such as divorce pulls out our emotional props and threatens our stability, equally strong forces within us seek to restore balance. In a creative divorce our renewed self-image is stronger and more independent than it was during our marriage, but in any case internal balance returns, life goes on, and we survive, sometimes in spite of ourselves.

Then there is the healing power of everyday life. The daily accomplishments, compliments from a neighbor, a "well done" from an employer, or just the completion of an unpleasant chore—they are telling us, if we would only listen, that we are coping successfully. Sometimes a friend's perceptive remark can radically change our perspective on our own situation. Alice, 27 and divorced after five years of marriage, had been suffering intense feelings of guilt for leaving the marriage. Nice girls, as her mother was constantly pointing out to her, didn't leave their husbands. One day she bumped into a friend at a bookstore who observed that Alice was lucky to have gotten out of a very bad marriage at such an early age, and with no children to worry about. "She said I had my whole life before me and the freedom to live it happily," Alice exclaimed. "It blew my mind. There I was feeling sorry for myself and moaning about the tragedy of my life. But I started thinking about what she said, and she's right. Staying in that marriage would have destroyed me, no matter what my mother says. It's my life and I have to live it."

Many people have such negative attitudes toward themselves and such unrealistically high standards that what they have accomplished never seems as important as what they haven't. This kind of thinking shuts off an important source of self-esteem. If you wash the kitchen floor and it looks good, permit yourself some pride in a job well done. Your message to yourself should be, "I washed the floor and it looks good," not "I washed the floor, but the rest of the house is still dirty and anyway all I'm good for is washing floors." When someone gives you a compliment on your appearance or for something you did, accept it as an honest expression of how at least one outsider views you. If you try to ferret out the "real" (i.e., negative) meaning behind every accolade you will end up like the man who told me, "If three people compliment me on a new tie, and one of them twitches while he's talking, I forget the compliments and remember the twitch."

Our most important resource, however, is our own past

history of dealing with the crises, large and small, which life throws our way. By the time we reach adulthood, we have all learned how to come to terms with our environment. We have gone to school; made important decisions; worked; raised a family; made other people happy. For many of us, divorce was not the first crisis of major proportions in our lives; we have had others, and we have overcome them. And even in the depths of divorce when we feel totally helpless, a part of us continues to function at work, in the community, with family and friends.

When we emerge successfully from the process of mourning, we can begin to recognize these abilities—not as new, but as the product of our life histories. For some people, such as Dolores, these are abilities we may never have known we possessed or, if we did know, downgraded them out of a feeling that they were inappropriate to our identities as husbands or wives. Dolores, who had always played the role of dependent wife and mother, felt inadequate as a single woman. Yet consider the responsibility, initiative, and drive she displayed every day of her life. Where did the abilities come from? They certainly did not spring up overnight. Rather they were the fruits of her entire life, including the years she had spent deferring to her husband. Even then she was making decisions every day about important matters—raising children, running a household, dealing with trades-people, arranging her family's schedule—although she probably never accorded them much importance while she was married. Now, as a single woman, she is able to cope quite successfully with a daily schedule that many others would not be up to.

What has happened is that she has transferred these abilities, which she always had, to the new demands of school and work. Her reluctance to admit their existence or grant their importance is a hangover from her not quite extinct self-image of the dependent wife who is not "supposed" to be so self-reliant. Like so many other divorced women (and men), Dolores's task is not only to develop her capacities, but to give them new labels. Her attitude is somewhat similar to Marge's, a woman in her late twenties who had been divorced for a year. Marge appeared to the group to be a highly competent person who was well in control of her new life: she had made application for a government job overseas and, while she was waiting for the results, was having some extensive dental problems taken care of that she had put off during the last years of her marriage. When the members of the group expressed approval of Marge's plans, she professed ignorance of the source of her "newfound" decisiveness.

"I guess I'm a different person now," she said. "When I was married I was so flighty and impulsive. You know, on Wednesday I'd decide to volunteer my services at the mental health association and by Monday I'd be working. Frank never liked that. Once while he was away on business I had the whole downstairs recarpeted. We had agreed months before to do it, but he never got around to making the arrangements, so I did it. Did he hit the ceiling when he got home!"

In fact, as the group pointed out, her behavior before and after her marriage was not all that different. What was different was her interpretation of it. The group could pick from Marge's story the common thread of a woman who knows what she wants and has the ability to get it. Yet for Marge-the-married-woman to accept this behavior she had to label it "flighty and impulsive," because she had grown up to believe that wives should always defer to husbands on important matters. She did her best to live up to this ideal. Rather than admit the abilities she had which negated it, she thought of them as signs of impulsiveness. After all, her thinking ran, it's acceptable for a woman to be considered flighty and impulsive, but being decisive and forthright smacks too much of domineering and bossy behavior.

Sometimes, when tunnel vision blinds divorced men and women to everything except their own "failure," I ask them to write down what they consider to be their outstanding talents, abilities, and strong points. The results are invariably impressive, to themselves and others: practicality, interest in people, drive to be productive and useful, responsibility, adaptability, persistence, good organization skills, patience, planning sense, mechanical ability, good memory, artistic expression—these are just a few of the qualities they mention. As we share these compilations, members of the group recognize in others' lists attributes of their own to which they have ascribed negative labels because they seem somehow inappropriate to their sex. Women members are encouraged to recognize such qualities as leadership and drive which they have displayed in their work as mothers, wives, and members of their community. Men often come to appreciate that what they thought of as a "good business sense" is often simply a sensitivity to the feelings of other people—not only a "feminine" but a "human" trait.

Many divorced people, particularly women, are still all too willing to accept their ex-spouses' negative evaluations of them as unarguable truth. I remember Pam, a forty-two-year-old woman who had believed she was stupid because her husband always told her so. "Nothing I ever did was right, as far as he was concerned," she said. "When I left he told me I'd regret it, because I was so ignorant I couldn't cross the street by myself. You'll be back, he said. What a laugh! I've been living alone for a year now, and I've got a good job, and I got it by myself. Sure I was stupid—stupid for living with a man like that for twenty years! And do you know what I was doing all the time while he was calling me stupid? Raising three children, running the house, keeping his real estate accounts, and managing two laundromats he bought—hiring people, paying the bills, working part time. But up until the time I left him I really thought I was the idiot he said I was."

RETHINKING VALUES
AND PRIORITIES

At that springtime meeting of my seminar Christine, 26, said, "I didn't really *do* anything over the Easter holidays, but a funny thing happened that got me thinking. In fact, I can see now I'm going to be thinking for a long time. I was talking with a friend of mine about a movie my husband and I had seen last year, right before we were divorced. I found myself saying, 'We didn't like it much.' And then I stopped. What did I mean, *we*? It's *I* now. And I liked that movie! And what's more, I don't like bourbon! And I don't like skiing! And I *do* like musical comedies!

"I feel like a lifelong Republican who suddenly switches to the Democratic party. I've got so much rethinking to do. Not just the little likes and dislikes we shared as a couple that I thought were mine, but the bigger things, too. I mean, if I went along with just a little thing for so many years like pretending to like skiing when it really bores me to death, what about some of my basic values? I can see a whole new person to discover behind the facade of "wife" and it's exciting! I don't have any earth-shaking answers to report yet, but I'm looking forward to the challenge of coming up with some."

Christine's moment of truth parallels the experience of Herb, 46, who had devoted all his time and energy to working for a large accounting concern during the twenty-three years of his marriage. "When we split up, the bottom dropped out of my work, along with everything else," he said. "I learned to my great surprise that I didn't like my job any more; I had sort of gone along with my wife who liked the security. I'm still working, but I'm looking around for something a little more venturesome where I can be with people. Opening a little restaurant, maybe."

Often a divorce is triggered by a discontent which, when acted upon, sets in motion a burst of personal growth that was not originally anticipated. Jill, 31, the mother of a two-year-old girl and the former wife of an up-and-coming advertising executive, entered into her marriage with every intention of being superwife. "I did the whole bit—the complete homemaker, the woman-be-hind-the-man, the powerhouse-in-her-own-right—but I felt bored and suffocated. When we separated I was in my second year of architecture school and I let Peter keep Linda. He had moved back in with his parents, and I just couldn't cope with my class schedule and Linda, too. When the divorce became final, I agreed for him to have permanent custody. I can see now I wasn't cut out to be a wife and mother. I love Linda, but I don't think that just because I carried her I'm necessarily the most perfect mother for her. The first months I really took myself over the coals. Guilty, guilty, guilty! I thought I must be some kind of freak to be able to give up my daughter like that. But now I know, feeling as I do, that I would only have been harming myself and my daughter if I had kept her. I'm not suggesting every woman follow my example, but I'm convinced I've done the right thing for me and my family."

Not many divorced men or women will experience such profound changes in their personal or professional lives as Herb and Jill. For most of us the process is one of slow and subtle reorderings. Without renouncing housework or motherhood completely, many women readjust their standards around the house. One woman, divorced for three years and now working as a personnel manager, put it this way: "When I look back at my immaculate house, I wonder what I was trying to prove. That place was so clean they could have performed open-heart surgery on the kitchen table with no fear of infection. Now things are clean enough. I don't have to worry about the city inspector, but my mental health is more important to me than the dust on the picture frames. Who has time for that any more?"

Lois, 39, measured the change in her values by her change in attitude toward her ex-husband. "First I cried all the time," she said, "and hoped he would come back. Also, I thought it would be better for the kids if I didn't have to work and could give them more time. But then I would think back on what life was like when he was here—the screaming, the criticism, the down-to-the-minute daily routine he insisted on. I couldn't even visit my friends without his permission. My place was in the home.

"About two months ago he split up with his girl friend and started calling me up and telling me how much he really loved me, and suggested maybe we could get back together again. I vacillated the first time or two he called, but when I realized that I would have to give up everything I have now for him and that miserable 'life' we had together, I almost vomited. So the last time he called I said no, definitely no, and told him to stop calling. I had a shaky moment or two afterward, but just for a few minutes. I could never live that way again—not with him or any other man. I've grown up too much since then."

TO BE ASSERTIVE:
I AM ME

One of the most positive signs of personal growth in divorced people is their willingness to give higher priority to their own interests and pleasures. For many of them, marriage was a series of sacrifices which depleted their own self-esteem. When they begin to value their own needs and act on them without feeling guilty and selfish, they begin to feel better about themselves and other people, and are in a better position to make the most of their own abilities. People with "doormat" written all over them get walked on; indeed, they invite trespass. They then feel victimized and put upon, angry with themselves for their spinelessness, and with others for taking advantage of them.

The ability to be assertive—to express yourself directly, honestly, spontaneously, and effectively—is vital to every situation you face as a divorced person: planning a new career, moving into the world of work, establishing your priorities, making friends with yourself and with others, handling your children, and enjoying mature relationships with members of the opposite sex.

Assertion is often confused with aggression, but in fact the two are completely different. Being assertive implies forcefulness only; aggression implies forcefulness *and* hostility. Although many women equate assertiveness with being pushy and unfeminine, it is really nothing more than the effective expression of all one's thoughts and feelings. Assertiveness includes the ability to express "positive" as well as "negative" feelings, the capacity to initiate action as well as the freedom to set limits for oneself and let others know what they are. An assertive person is able to say to someone, "What you did made me feel angry," without putting the other person down. An aggressive person intrudes on others. He or she says, "How stupid you are for having done that!" The distinction, sometimes subtle in practice but nevertheless extremely important, is often blurred in the minds of those people who hesitate to say what they really feel in the belief that it would be considered aggressive, impolite, or unfriendly.

"Actually, many people don't know how to stand up for their rights without being aggressive," according to Pamela Butler, a behavioral psychologist who conducts assertive training groups at the Behavior Therapy Institute in Sausalito, California. "As a result they hold their feelings inside and let them fester. It's a problem common to many marriages. In such a situation two outcomes are possible. Either some 'minor' detail eventually provokes a savage (and apparently irrational) attack, causing the wounded party to lash back and making the attacker feel guilty for the outburst. Or—and this is worse—the feelings will be turned inward. When this happens, the person withdraws emotionally and sometimes physically. He or she becomes bitter and resentful. In some cases not expressing feelings when they occur may inhibit the capacity to function sexually. It can also help trigger depression and psychosomatic illnesses."

In the course of her research Dr. Butler has observed important differences in the areas where men and women have difficulty asserting themselves. "Women find it easier than men to express positive feelings, to say 'I like you.' Men tend to view expressions of love or tenderness as evidence of weak and therefore unmasculine behavior. On the other hand, women have a harder time than men expressing negative feelings, venturing opinions, and setting limits for themselves. Our culture has given them the idea that assertion in these areas is bitchy, bossy, and unfeminine. Interestingly, I have found that just as many men as women have difficulties in initiating contact, that is, talking to a stranger, asking for something, establishing a relationship with the opposite sex."

Not asserting oneself can lower one's self-esteem. "Rather than say no, a woman will often find it easier to go along with something she really doesn't like," Dr. Butler says, "but in doing so she will have diminished her view of herself. Men suffer from the inability to set limits, too. One man told me he was afraid to refuse his boss' offer of another drink because he thought it might cost him his job.

"In fact, when you let someone know your limits and feelings you are doing both of you a service. You are telling yourself that you are a person with rights and privileges, and you are making life a lot more pleasant for the other person. A wife who doesn't like vacations in the mountains may never tell her husband directly, but she makes sure in a hundred little ways that he knows it."

Expressing one's feelings at the time they occur also paves the way for compromise. One woman who had consented to postpone separation from her husband until their son's wedding found that, despite their agreement to live temporarily "together but separately," she became hurt and angry when her husband would come home from the office, eat dinner with his family, and then proceed to shower and dress for a date with another woman. Rather than say nothing and seethe inwardly, she should have told him how she felt. Not "You bastard! How can you be so insensitive?" but something like, "I know we agreed to this arrangement, but it still hurts me to have you eat with us and then see you get ready to go out with someone else." They might then have been able to work out another arrangement, perhaps one in which he left for a date directly from work. Maybe the solution wouldn't have been quite so simple in this case, but she could never know without telling him how she feels.

In her assertive training groups Dr. Butler tries to get participants to recognize the importance of even a small assertive act. "Many people have learned to be critical of themselves," she says. "We say things to ourselves that we would never say to other people. Maybe it's because we were taught as children that praising ourselves was bad. Then, too, many people adopt the ploy of downgrading something they did in the hopes that someone will be around to say, 'Oh, no. You really did a good job.' Whatever the reason, continual self-punishment is harmful, and in the training groups we try to counteract this tendency by making people stop and take note of every small accomplishment. Too often people refuse to recognize any achievement short of their ultimate goal."

Many times people set goals which are impossibly difficult to attain; they become a means of escape from the present. If, for example, a man or woman says, "I'll never be able to become a doctor at my age, so what's the use of going back to school and trying for a new career?" he or she is giving up before starting. This attitude precludes other career choices which may be more easily attainable.

One of Dr. Butler's major interests is the relationship between women's assertive abilities and the women's movement today. "Some people believe that if discriminatory hiring and promotion practices against women suddenly ended, women would immediately move into positions of greater responsibility in the business and professional world, but I don't think it is quite that simple," Dr. Butler claims. "You are still left with the fact that women assert themselves less than men. Studies have shown that, in meetings involving men and women, women talk less than men, offer fewer opinions, interrupt less often, and permit themselves to be interrupted more. It's not that they don't have the ability to lead or be forceful, but that they fear that by expressing the full range of their competency and power they will appear unfeminine and bossy."

Helping women assert themselves more, Dr. Butler has found, means working with them in situations requiring disagreement or the expression of anger. "We take it step by step," she reports, "often from a list they prepare of situations in their own lives which present the greatest problems." The following is a typical list starting with the easiest and proceeding to the most difficult situation:

- entering and leaving a room
- making small talk with a man
- initiating a conversation with a man, then holding it for a prolonged period
- asserting myself with clerks and waitresses
- stating an opinion that differs from another's, then not backing down
- accepting criticism
- disagreeing with someone
- expressing anger if I am unjustly put down

- arguing with another person
- expressing intense anger with my husband

"Sometimes I begin by going around the room and asking people to read from a list of assertive statements," Dr. Butler says, "just so they become aware of the importance of tone of voice, eye contact, and facial expression. This exercise can be a revelation to women who feel the sky will fall in if they say something assertively without apologizing or smiling. I remember one woman who had the statement, 'This is a ticket line. Would you mind going to the end?' She had to read it twice before she really sounded and looked like she meant what she said. When the group complimented her on her forceful delivery the second time, she said, 'But didn't I sound awfully bitchy?' Armed with the group's assurance that she didn't sound bitchy at all, she felt more confident to assert herself on more important issues in her own life. And the positive reactions of others helped her clarify the differences between assertive and aggressive behavior."

Assertion is required of the divorced person who would live creatively in the present, more assertion, in fact, than people who lead unchanging lives have to display. Life for the divorced man or woman is at first a void. To fill the void with other than meaningless activity or excessive duties and obligations to others, he or she must be able to act on his or her own interests. The demands on women of living singly often require new attitudes toward things they may have never done before—writing checks, balancing the budget, managing assets, carrying out household repairs, driving a car. These are not masculine or feminine tasks, but survival necessities. Yet many women continue to label them "unfeminine" in order to avoid the responsibility of living in the present. However, with every tiny risk, with every small move toward assertion of their own interests, they are strengthening a positive self-image as single people.

One of the most positive by-products of the women's movement for social and economic equality has been the creation of a climate supportive of women's efforts to discover and take charge of themselves—their bodies, their lives, their own fulfillment. A prime contributor to this change has been women's discussion, or consciousness-raising groups, in which women have gained the confidence of knowing that other women feel as they do, that they are not freaks or deviants because their personal needs and feelings do not fit the cultural stereotype of their sex. Other women embark on their own voyages of self-discovery. Each act of assertion moves them farther toward the goal of finding out what kind of person they really are behind the female roles they have played.

For women whose entire lives had been given meaning through relationships to men—fathers, boyfriends, husbands, bosses—it comes as a pleasant, if sometimes unsettling, surprise to discover that they don't need men as much as they did in the past. They don't need to borrow their husbands' successes to feel worthwhile, nor do they need the approval of a man to feel good about themselves. Once they begin to understand and respect themselves as independent people, they can sort out the fulfilling from the demeaning dependencies on the men in their lives. This knowledge works to the men's advantage as well. Once they no longer feel burdened with the crushing responsibility of having to be "everything" to their wives or friends, they can begin to move away from masculine stereotypes toward greater expression of their own individuality.

Many women today are reporting striking changes in their attitudes toward other women. A young mother in one of my seminars who was considering resuming her maiden name said it this way: "For the first time in my life I have actually made friends with other women. I no longer see them as competitors for some man's attention. I have found that I can get support from other women that a man could never give. I'm no man-hater. But I can see why a man might be jealous to know that a woman is not totally reliant on him. Maybe that's why you read so many charges in the press that the women's movement is basically lesbian."

MAKING CHOICES IN THE WORLD OF WORK

The ability to be assertive can clarify the career-planning process which many divorced women are faced with. A woman aware of her full powers (even if, like Dolores, this awareness is only partly conscious) has the confidence to seek out the kind of work that she will find fulfilling instead of falling into something stultifying. Furthermore, anyone—man or woman—who knows what he or she wants is less likely to be coerced by the expectations of family, friends, and society at large.

The assertive person will take a realistic view of the job market and, if the economy is depressed or discrimination against women is in evidence, will take even an unsatisfying job, if necessary, and use it as a stepping stone to something better. Such a person was Lillian, 37, divorced after a fourteen-year marriage. Needing an income but finding that her B.A. in history was of little value in today's job market, she took a position as a secretary in a bank. She liked the banking business but detested the typing and was determined to get out of the secretarial ghetto. She joined a women's group sponsored by her local chapter of the National Organization for Women. As a result of the confidence she gained through NOW, she got up the nerve to ask for a raise. And two years later, when an opening for an assistant manager came up, she applied for the job and got it.

"I almost didn't apply, because I was sure it was reserved for a man," she said. "But companies are worried about their discrimination against women, and are beginning to take women seriously. But now that I've got this job, I'm taking some courses in administration which the bank sponsors for its employees. I don't see any reason why I shouldn't be branch manager some day. Five years ago I wouldn't have dreamed I'd have come as far as I have."

Sometimes insights into our real interests and needs, as well as exposure to rewarding careers, are found in out-of-the-way places. Take the case of Jeanette, 31. Divorced after ten years of being a housewife, she now had to have a job, as much from emotional as financial necessity. "I wanted a paying job," she said. "Not that I hadn't worked hard all during the marriage, but in this society earning money is a tangible sign that you're worth something and I want that feeling." Jeanette's problem was that, although she came from a background which disapproved of women working anywhere but the office or the classroom, she did not have the skills or the interest for that kind of work.

Her solution was accidental, but it illustrates the point that we can learn about ourselves from many different kinds of work experience. "A friend of mine who owns a restaurant happened to tell me that one of his waitresses had gotten sick," Jeanette said. "So on a fluke I volunteered to help out, and I discovered I really liked the job—meeting the public, getting physical exercise, responding well in moments of pressure. Now I'm there on a regular basis five evenings a week. My family is furious that their daughter with a college degree in English literature is doing 'menial' work, but I love it. And it's opened up a whole career field I hadn't known about before. Did you know that there are a lot of conference centers around here for business executives who want to hold meetings and seminars? The restaurant manager told me of one that was looking for a banquet director and I think I may apply."

Although there is a tendency to think that it is only the divorced women who must think about a new career, I have known many men whose divorce was the catalyst for a major occupational change. To a certain extent this was my experience, in that I switched from a job as an employment and career counselor with a state agency to being a self-employed divorce adjustment counselor. Far more dramatic is the story of Joe Roberts, 47, who left twenty-five years in the business world behind and became a college teacher.

I first met Joe in private counseling sessions two weeks after he had left his wife of twenty-one years and their two sons, aged eighteen and twenty. "Don't get the idea there was another woman," he said. "It's just that we were no longer the same people we were when we got married. While the kids were around, we managed to avoid the fact that we didn't much like each other any more, but when they left we had to face it. We argued about every little thing as if it were a matter of war and peace. The final straw was some ridiculous fight over why didn't I put the cheese back in the refrigerator when I was through? No, I've had it. Period."

Yet behind his bravado was a man in crisis: "It's like part of me died! We inflicted so much pain on each other." In these early sessions Joe wept frequently and without shame in honest expression of his vulnerability and fear. As he was later to learn, by allowing himself full expression of his humanity without fearing this was unmanly, Joe emerged from the mourning process a stronger person: "I found out I had more things going for me than I thought I had when I first separated."

Joe's divorce crisis led him to rethink the values and priorities which had governed the last twenty-one years of his life. Married early and with a rapidly growing family to support. Joe had had to drop out of a master's degree program in sociology and go to work. He took a job as a salesman for a wholesale furniture house and for the last fourteen years had been its sales manager. The pay was good, and he had a fine record, but after his divorce work began to seem unbearable. "I guess I stayed there for the family," he admitted. "Or that's what I told myself so I wouldn't have to face up to the fact that I didn't like the work itself. And I really hated it. I always had the feeling that I was conning people into deals, and it made me feel slimy inside. I tried to get my kicks through money—a new car every year or two, a big house, being the richest guy on the block. Well, hell, if money is all life has to offer I might as well jump off a bridge tomorrow. I've got to do whatever it is that makes me feel life is worth living."

What Joe wanted to do was return to his interest in sociology, finish his master's degree, and become a college teacher. However the thought of going back to school terrified him. "What would people think of a forty-seven-year-old in the classroom? I'd stick out like a sore thumb. And how could I compete with all these sharp young kids? Don't you think I'm pretty long in the tooth for that?"

I was happy to be able to contradict Joe on both counts. Colleges and universities have witnessed a tremendous boom in adult enrollment during the last decade and every sign points to further growth in the future: increased leisure time, greater job obsolescence, and the simple desire of people to learn more about themselves and the rapidly changing world they live in. Adults in colleges and universities today can be found enrolled for basic and advanced degrees, participating in industry-sponsored training programs, or simply sampling courses in areas of personal interest. The blue-collar blues are not peculiar only to factory workers: men and women in every kind of job are seeking, in fact demanding, personal satisfaction from their work, and further education is one means to this end. Colleges, mindful of this interest, have adapted their programs and teaching methods to attract more adults. A man or woman returning to school today after a twenty-year absence would be surprised by higher-education's new flexibility—innovative degree programs, high-quality evening and weekend classes, independent study options, and provisions to grant credit for previous work experience. Where a college once expected a student, no matter what his background or previous education, to take a prescribed series of courses in order to get a degree, more and more institutions today are permitting the student to design his own program of study, in cooperation with a faculty adviser. Such programs can include a mix of classroom instruction, on-the-job training, independent reading and study, and directed field work. Schedules are changing, too: some colleges have adult programs that meet only on weekends or during the summer months—and some institutions have devised programs in which a student may earn a degree without ever setting foot on campus.

As for Joe's fear that he was too old to learn, studies have confirmed what colleges and universities learned with the influx of veterans from the Second World War: adults with motivation, maturity, and sense of purpose can do better in school than many traditional college-age students. As Joe himself realized, in his personal and professional life he had developed abilities which would stand him in good stead as a student and teacher: intelligence, self-discipline, a passionate interest in social and political ideas, and an enthusiastic and engaging personality through which to communicate this interest.

Encouraged by this knowledge, Joe acted on his interest, quit his job, and enrolled full time in a master's degree program in sociology. He knew the risks—the scarcity of teaching jobs today, the difficulty of getting back into the business world if he decided not to complete the program—but he decided to go for broke. "If this doesn't work out," he said, "it's still better than spending the rest of my life in that job." Even though he had to reduce his standard of living drastically when he went back to school, he found that once he had made the decision he felt happier and stronger than he had in years. "Once I decided to enroll, I felt so excited and free just not having to fight off thinking about what it was I really wanted out of life."

Two years later Joe received his degree. As he reported during our occasional meetings, it wasn't all smooth sailing. "At first I thought everyone was pointing at the old man in the classroom and thinking he should be out holding down a job. But then it changed. I suppose I got tired of racing out of class at the end of the lecture to avoid personal contact with the students. It dawned on me that I was avoiding them rather than the other way around. So I decided to just act like me and try to get to know them. What did I have to lose? Well, that was the big breakthrough, and I found that those youngsters were interesting and decent people. Some have become real good friends of mine. It's not your age that matters, it's your attitude about your age."

Joe admitted to some adjustment problems to an academic schedule in the first few months, but he kept plugging away and at graduation was among the top five students in his class. "I was rusty at first," he remembers, "but I found I used my time much more efficiently than I did when I was in college before. I didn't have the time to fool around. This was my big chance, and I wanted to make the most of it."

The last time I saw Joe he had gotten a job in a community college as a sociology teacher, after six months of looking. Job hunting was just about as rough as he thought it would be, but his past business experience and the ability to present himself well in an interview worked to his advantage. The college that hired him was looking for someone with nonacademic experience as well as the proper teaching credentials, and selected him from a field of forty applicants. "It's a real turn-on getting paid for doing what you like," he said, looking happier and years younger than when I first met him. "Even though my present salary is just exactly one-third of what I was making before, I'm three times—no, make that one hundred times—happier. I feel great, I've made a hell of a lot of new friends, and I wouldn't change places with anyone now for all the money in the world."

Joe's story is a story of choices—choices made in awareness of his own real needs and abilities. His ultimate happiness was not easily or quickly arrived at, but once he had made the decision to move with his feelings he released the emotional energy he needed to strive for his goal. The world of work, like the rest of life, is changing rapidly and presents more options than many people who are afraid of self-direction let themselves think about. New patterns of employment are emerging which permit women (and men) to blend domestic with work responsibilities. One plan which has received national attention calls for hiring two women to share one job, thereby tapping the large pool of qualified women who want rewarding work but cannot spend forty hours a week away from their families. Employers in this experiment report these women have better attendance records, greater enthusiasm, and do better work than employees who put in the standard forty-hour week.

GUIDELINES

To seize whatever new opportunities the future will bring—be they personal or occupational—we must be able to distinguish our real needs and abilities from those society has programmed for us. My own experience with members of my seminars has convinced me that the crisis of divorce can spark just such self-knowledge which, when acted upon, produces further personal growth. Plans for action will be different for each person as he or she begins to cope with new realities, but if they are based on the following guidelines, their chances for success will be greater:

1. Separate your *real* feelings and needs from what you think society is requiring of you as male and female role players.

2. Take tiny risks, and give yourself permission to make mistakes. An error-free life is a dead giveaway for zero personal growth.

3. Set realistic goals for yourself, and don't wait until the job is over before assessing your progress. Knowing how much you have accomplished will give you the boost you need to finish the task.

4. Consider the present as a series of choices, not inevitabilities. If circumstances force you temporarily into an unpleasant situation in your personal or professional life, learn what you can from it and begin to make plans to move ahead, rather than resigning yourself to permanent unhappiness and despair.

5. Don't underestimate the capacity for even the smallest act of self-assertion to enhance your own opinion of yourself as an independent single person.

6. Seek help when you need it—from family, friends, or from professionals. Life is not a test, and you aren't cheating when you request assistance from others.

These guidelines, distilled from the experiences of myself and the men and women I have counseled, can expand the lives of divorced people far beyond what they might once have settled for. They open up the possibility for the kind of life a woman once told me the women's movement had made possible for her: "The freedom to live up to my potential without being restricted by what society says I should or shouldn't do. The freedom to express all my feelings, even the angry feelings, because I do get angry. The freedom to take responsibility for my own life and not have it determined only by my relationship with other people. The freedom to let other people be themselves and to enjoy them for what they are, because I am secure in my knowledge of who I am."

CHAPTER 6

New Ways of Relating to People

A creative divorce provides the opportunity to define relationships with other people by living them instead of by forcing them to fit a preconceived set of expectations. Each new experience you enter into enlarges your capacity for additional experiences, and reinforces your thrust toward living in the present which began with separation. Out of the suffering of those initial months has begun to emerge an awareness of the person behind the facade of husband or wife. As you come to accept and to *like* that single man or woman you will notice substantial changes in how you look at others—family, friends of long standing, and new people in your life. More secure in the knowledge of who you are you will start to separate out the fulfilling from the demeaning dependencies on others and can begin to enjoy people for themselves.

Part and parcel of this process is a marked change in values, a restructuring of the premises we have lived by during the years of our marriages and even before. The shift is from the superficial to the substantial, from externals to internals, from "I should" to "I am," from rigidity to flexibility, from obligation to experimentation. Here is what people in my seminars have discovered:

People are more important than material goods. As a divorced man put it, "The biggest change in my life is the fact that I now make a point of being with people who re-

146

ally mean something to me—my kids, my friends. Before the divorce it was work first and people second. But what's the use of having a big house, new car, and a color TV if you have no one to share experiences with or love or just have fun with? Now I know what the poet meant when he said that life is an affair of people."

People are appreciated for themselves instead of for their appearance, wealth, or membership in a particular age or social class. This change is often the direct result of having been burned in a marriage which was based primarily on one or more of these surface attributes. Because people in a creative divorce have come to realize the importance of their own feelings, they are more sensitive to the need for making contact with other people at this "feeling" level, and are therefore less likely to enter into new relationships based on the same old attitudes. A classic illustration of this shift in values was provided by a woman who told the group, "When I married Joe, I was the envy of all my friends. He was handsome, a sharp dresser, and always had the latest-model car. What a catch! But I learned. Nine years of his egotism, total non-communication, lousy sex—boy, did I learn! No more of that for me. All he did was work, work, work. Now I want someone to play with me."

They begin to see themselves as separate, many-faceted individuals worthy of respect and love. Perhaps the greatest benefit of a creative divorce is an enhanced sense of self-esteem—not just for our rational faculties, but for our emotional and physical selves as well. In the beginning stages of separation, we began to move toward this awareness when we accepted the feelings of anxiety, guilt, and anger inside us as ours—and no one else's—and began to put them to positive use. The process toward wholeness continued when we started to apply skills and abilities which we hadn't known we possessed to new problems of single life. The more we explore and test out these often unfamiliar parts of ourselves, the more we fold them into our notion of who we are. As a forty-year-old man said, "I like *me*—not just my head or my strength, but the whole bag—the tears, the fears, the weakness, too. Now when I have 'mixed emotions' about something, I try to figure out what the different parts of me are saying, rather than squelching them. Maybe this is why I am so much more open to people than I once was. A scary feeling, sometimes, but really the only way to live. Before there was a plastic shield between me and the rest of the world."

They begin to see other people as people, and not as extensions of their own needs and fantasies. Because so many of the men and women in my seminars chalk up their divorces to the fact that they married images rather than people, they are determined not to let it happen again. I have heard variations on the following story time and again: "When my husband asked for a divorce, I was completely floored—not only by what he said but by the fact that he suddenly seemed like a totally different person. I realized I didn't really know him at all, that without my being aware of it, he had changed over the years. Maybe I *never* knew him."

As many divorced people learn, basing a marriage on immature needs can lead to trouble when one partner matures faster than the other. One forthright woman said, "My husband didn't marry me, he married his idea of a cute little girl. And I played right into it. The only trouble was I stopped wanting to be his cute little girl. I guess I was growing up. Anyway, I changed somehow, but he didn't. Now when I meet someone new I try to see the whole person, not just the parts that fit my fantasy." When you are secure enough with yourself so that you don't need people in a childish way, you can see so much more in them. Once you stop using them as mirrors for your own fantasies, you see another world beyond. As one woman said, "It's a through-the-looking-glass experience."

LIVING ALONE
VS. LIVING LONELY

Although loneliness usually tops the list of problems for divorced men and women, in its deepest sense this feeling has little to do with living alone. It is quite common to many marriages. Two can be just as lonely a number as one. The wife upstairs in bed and the husband falling asleep in front of the late-late show; the wife in the kitchen and the husband in the living room hiding behind his newspaper; the wife and husband talking *only* about matters concerning their children: what could be lonelier than this kind of alienation?

We all know that people can be lonely in a crowd, but in the first months of a divorce we still tend to blame all our lonely feelings on the fact that we are living alone. We miss the warm body in bed, the small talk, the accustomed routine, even the fights. If only someone was there, we think, we wouldn't be lonely any more. Our solution then becomes an escape into a frantic social life, or work, or relationships whose only real purpose is to keep us from being alone with our solitude.

Although these outlets can fill many gaps in our daily lives created by the absence of our spouse, they are not solutions to the basic cause of loneliness and, if followed to excess, can be more destructive than holing up in our house or apartment and refusing to see other people. To overcome our acute sense of loneliness, we must first understand that it springs from the feelings of deprivation and loss triggered by our separation. We feel at the outset that our emotional survival depends on others, not on ourselves, and when that support is withdrawn, loneliness is the desolating result. If we have lived during our marriages as if we were half-persons, this is not so much a new experience as it is a long-standing feeling which separation has intensified.

The answer, then, to this basic kind of loneliness is to continue the process of building self-esteem which began during the mourning process. When we start to flex our emotional muscles as independent people and gain confidence in our ability to take care of ourselves, two things start to happen which dissipate our loneliness and fear of solitude: we clarify the needs which we can fulfill ourselves from those which only others can meet, and we begin to like ourselves more. We stop thinking of moments of solitude as accusations of our worthlessness and start to welcome them as valuable periods for reflection and personal growth. Instead of feeling them thrust upon us, we see them as quiet times of our own choosing, necessary pauses in which we recharge our batteries and come to greater understanding of the changes that are taking place within us.

When you feel comfortable with yourself, being alone gives you the time to renew old friendships. Felice, a diminutive woman in her late fifties, sets aside a five o'clock cocktail hour on afternoons when she is home. "I fix myself one martini—just one—and set it next to my 'hot line.' That's what I call my red telephone. Then I call up one or two friends here in the city or around the country. Nothing long-winded, just a short visit to see how they are and let them know what I'm doing. They're busy with their own lives, just as I am with mine, so I'm not upset if sometimes they can't talk. It's a lovely way to break the daily routine."

This is the time for healing friendship-fractures. As I was to learn, once you are secure with yourself as a separate person, you can understand that every rejection is not a rejection of you, that your friends have their own concerns to worry about which influence the way they behave. When we do manage to take the initiative and reach out to old friends, the results are almost always gratifying.

Helga, 37, loved to square-dance; for many years she and her husband had been mainstays of the local community dance group. After her divorce, however, she felt so squeamish about seeing these people that she would drive for two hours to another town which had square-dancing activities. "It wasn't because I thought I would see my ex-husband," she said. "He had moved out of state. The thing was that the group was made up totally of married people, friends we had known only as couples. I thought people would give me the cold shoulder if I showed up with a new partner, so I just stayed away. But one night the car broke down and my friend and I couldn't make it to the other group, so we decided to take the chance and go to the one here in town. Well, I was welcomed back with open arms! *They* thought *I* was being standoffish. It's been just wonderful to be there again, and to know that my fears were only in my head. They say I look so much happier now. One woman took me aside and said they had all known something was wrong long before we separated. And I thought no one else could have guessed."

Relatives and ex-relatives can seem to present a particularly thorny problem, until tested out. A man in one of my seminars was perplexed over the fact that he wanted to keep in touch with his sister-in-law and her family, with whom he had become good friends during his marriage, but hesitated to call her up out of fear that she would naturally side with his ex-wife. But because he wanted so much to maintain the friendship, he took the risk of calling up and was enormously pleased that she was glad to hear from him. She, too, had been suffering qualms about how she should behave and for that reason had not gotten in touch with him. They have since resumed their friendship with no feelings of guilt or disloyalty on either side, and it is just as enjoyable as it was before. Also, he finds that continuing his link with his wife's family through his sister-in-law provides a kinship link important to his children's emotional adjustment to his divorce. "Don't get me wrong," he said, "I wouldn't do it just for that reason alone, but it is an added benefit."

Many of the members of my group, especially women, report a great reluctance to tell their parents about their divorce. In the initial stages they feel that their parents will blame them for having separated. Although I have known a few instances in which this has happened, I know of many more in which the son or daughter was pleasantly surprised by parental understanding. Once they take the risk, they find that their parents are people, too, with unexpected capacities to understand and show compassion.

Roberta, 30, held off telling her parents until three months after her husband had moved out. "The first thing my father asked me was if I had done everything I could to save the marriage," she said. "And when I told him I had, then he accepted my decision. My mother said she was vastly relieved. She knew even before I did that things weren't going well! I suppose it all boils down to the fact that when parents see their children suffer, even the most conservative will prefer divorce to continued pain. Since I had that talk with my parents, my mother and I have opened up a lot more with each other. If only she had been able to come out earlier with some of the things she's told me recently about her own marriage, I might have been in a better position to understand my own. I thought their marriage was perfect, but it turns out they have just as many problems as the rest of us."

WHO NEEDS ANOTHER ADOLESCENCE?

A creative divorce signals a period of experimentation with new ways of relating to other people. People coming out of a bad marriage know they don't want a repetition of the past. As a result of the self-awareness gained during the mourning process, they have a better idea now of what it will take to make them happy. Some of their findings about themselves seem new at first, but in fact they are simply aspects of themselves which had been buried during their marriages. Now they have the opportunity, unencumbered by extensive commitments and obligations, to test out their independent personalities in a variety of relationships with many other people. Free from their initial desperation to find a fast replacement for their missing half, they can start looking around them and experiencing pleasure with other people for its own sake, and not as the first step toward remarriage.

The difference between this attitude and husband- or wife-hunting is immense. As one woman said, "When I started going out again after my divorce, I kept my eye firmly fixed on marriage potential. I was uptight all the time. The most casual dinner or movie date became a testing ground: what kind of father would he be, how reliable was he, what kind of couple did we make? I never let myself have a good time. But the more I begin to enjoy my single life, the less I feel as if I *have* to get married. Now I find I am following up with friendships because of the pleasure they provide, and I've met many different kinds of men I like. Not all as husband material, certainly, but there are many kinds of commitments to other people, and not every one has to lead to marriage to be worthwhile. It's not an all-or-nothing deal."

Experimentation during this period is an absolute necessity for many divorced men and women, according to Shirley Gehrke Luthman, codirector of the prestigious Family Therapy Institute in San Rafael, California, and author of the insightful book, *Intimacy: The Essence of Male and Female*. "Many of the men and women I counsel have gotten out of what was a bad marriage but a good family. By this I mean they had created, within their marriage, a family that was more reliable and beneficial than their original families. They could depend on each other in ways they never could depend on their parents. What often happens is that they finish their growing up in this new 'family' and then find that—while it may still be a good family—it may not be the marriage they want. It's important for them to appreciate the fact that they did create a good, useful family in which they could continue to grow, even though it did not evolve into a marriage which fit. That appreciation mitigates the feelings of failure when their marriage dissolves.

"When they divorce they find themselves for the first time in their lives at a point where they are ready to experiment with new ways of relating to the opposite sex. This is equally as true for women as it is for men. Just in the last two years I've noticed a tremendous change in the willingness of women to express their sensual and sexual selves without making the final commitment of marriage. When I consider the taboos they have operated under for so many years, I'm amazed that women can break out at all. It's a real tribute to the human organism.

"Unfortunately, thanks to society's past attitudes, many people find it difficult to accept responsibility for this kind of behavior. The only way they can try out new relationships is to think of themselves as helpless victims. When I see this happening with a woman—or a man—I usually try to get them to see how they have set up the situation to guarantee that they will be victimized. For example, if you go out and meet some guy and he turns out to be a real loser, just ask yourself, 'Why did I set that up?' Not with judgment, or even analytically, just the question, 'OK, I have choices to make, yet I sent out the vibes that attracted this guy. Why?'

"This is a big step. Most people don't take responsibility of this kind because they can't stop judging themselves. If they admit responsibility for having set up a situation in which they attract losers, they think they must be, in the words of a colleague of mine, either bad, sick, stupid, or crazy. They shouldn't put themselves down. All it really means is that there are parts of them they aren't aware of, not just their heads. To get in touch with all the different parts of you, you have to own them—without judgment, analysis, or pushing—just own it all, whatever happens to you. Once you recognize that you do have a choice, you touch some wellspring inside. OK, you say, I'm suffering. Why do I *choose* to suffer? When you come to this point, the answers arise spontaneously."

Mrs. Luthman believes that divorced men and women, especially after a long marriage, need a period of experimentation with a variety of different people and relationships before they commit themselves to another marriage. "It's a kind of emotional adolescence, really, time to be free just to *feel* and not worry about commitment or involvement or anything permanent. So many times people have tortured themselves toward the end of the marriages trying to make them work to the point that they feel drained and need to be filled up again. Their 'should' systems are so strong and self-punishing that they are literally empty emotionally. Now is the perfect time for them to focus on feeling good, to find out what they like. I tell them to do what they want to as long as it feels good, and to stop the minute it doesn't. Going with your feelings is the most nourishing, healing process there is: it really fills you up. It may take two months, six months, or longer, but one morning you wake up and you don't feel drained, you don't feel terrible, you don't feel like a failure—you may not feel like the greatest person in the world, either— but you feel there is something in your internal 'pot.' At this point reflection arises spontaneously, and you can begin to take a look at what you have learned about yourself and where you want to go from here."

When people begin to go only in the direction of what they enjoy—be it work, relationships with other people, or what they do from minute to minute—they will be heading toward "aliveness." "In my book I describe it as being turned on, experiencing an unblocked flow of energy within oneself, a supra-awareness to stimuli, a quality of letting go into the moment with an ability to experience the moment totally," Mrs. Luthman says. She has found that people experience aliveness in different ways. "Some people feel a tingling sensation, a weightlessness, a total investment. Others feel frightened. Really being alive can be frightening because it constantly takes you into situations where there are no accustomed external supports, no 'shoulds.' You are following your feelings, your intuition, and you have to trust them. No one can make this leap suddenly; you have to ease into it. The important thing is to know that this is where life is. You have a choice: you can be safe and partly dead, or you can be alive and risking all the time. However, it's been my experience that once people begin moving in this direction, they get hooked, and they can't go back. And you certainly can't separate sexuality and sensuality from aliveness. The more alive you are, the 'sexier' and more sensual you feel."

AT MY AGE?

"Dating" again! Is there any mature divorced man or woman who does not wince at that word or, worse, "boyfriend" and "girlfriend"? Early in my divorce I remember how shocked I was to overhear the daughter of a woman I was going out with refer to me as "Mom's boyfriend." Me, a boyfriend? It was absurd! And yet consider the alternatives: lover, suitor, beau, friend. Our language lags behind the times when it comes to providing labels for adults who are neither married nor monkish. Nothing seems to reflect a shade of meaning we are comfortable with: "lover" is too steamy and flamboyant for some tastes, "suitor" bespeaks a seriousness of purpose which may not be present, "beau" is a little quaint and in any case applies only to a man. Most of us fall back on 'friend," spoken with a certain weight and quickly followed by some pronoun to establish gender.

Yet in the decades ahead our language will be forced to accommodate itself to the double facts that a greater percentage of the population will fall in the over-forty age brackets, and that these people are not sitting on life's sidelines. Today one out of ten Americans is sixty-five or older, and if the birth rate continues to remain low, this proportion may increase in the next twenty-five years to one out of every five. Americans have been surprised in recent months to read about the existence of vigorous social and sexual activities in retirement communities. We may titter over the thought of grandma and grandpa sneaking off to the park for a quiet tryst, but they are being perfectly normal; it is our attitudes which will have to change.

Aging has been described as a crisis of the imagination, and as studies are proving, this is largely true. I have known many men who became quietly hysterical as their fortieth birthday drew near, because they believed it would mark the onset of impotence and the end of their chances for sex. The plight of the older woman in a society that values only the external feminine attributes of firm flesh, smooth skin, and shapely limbs needs no elaboration here. However, values are changing. Thanks in large part to the women's movement, we are slowly coming to the realization that an older woman can be just as attractive as an older man, that a sexually active older woman is not an obscenity, and that there is more to intimate relationships than external appearances. Studies of couples in their seventies have revealed that three out of four lead active sex lives. When we knock out our false assumption that people over forty (or fifty, or sixty) are sexually dead, we will all come to expect sexual fulfillment for as long as we live. Then the Dinah Shores, the Sybil Burtons, the Charlie Chaplins, and the Justice Douglases will cease to be the odd exceptions. We will enjoy other people because they are human beings we find compatible, not because they are of a particular age or type.

A major eye-opener for me has been the number of women in their thirties, forties, and above who have told me they feel free to enjoy the company of men younger than themselves. Partly, they say, it is the result of the wearing away of social taboos, but once they begin to accept the possibility, they find many men with whom they are compatible who happen to be younger. Rosemary, 44, told the group she has gone out with several men at least ten years younger than she is. "At first I was sure they were doing me a big favor," she admitted, "until one man told me it was a real pleasure to be with a grown-up woman who had a little something between the ears. Sure, I've met one or two who probably have some hang-up with their mothers, but I could accept it and still enjoy our relationship on its own terms. Maybe it's the way they were raised, but I find that younger men are more willing to consider me as a person. Talking and sharing are important to them. So many older men seem to think I'm just another opportunity to prove their masculinity. They come on so strong I turn off."

During this period a divorced person may be doing a lot of growing up, and the kinds of people he or she goes out with will mirror this growth. Many middle-aged men will seek out the company of younger women, not primarily because of physical appeal or to prove they are still young, but out of a need to find someone whose emotional maturity matches their own. If, for example, a forty-five-year-old man is just beginning to define himself according to what he finds inside rather than by an external set of standards or obligations, he may discover his emotional maturity parallels that of a twenty-year-old girl who has grown up free of a strong "should" system and is therefore more knowledgeable about her own feelings. The possibility, of course, is that the man, with his additional years of life experience, may catch up with and eventually surpass the younger woman's emotional growth. However, no two people grow at the same rate or the same time, even if they are the same chronological age. In this time of experimentation, there is nothing wrong with pairings between two people of divergent ages, since the whole purpose is to explore further the kind of person you are becoming without feeling the need to make any permanent commitment. If the relationship becomes permanent, so be it; otherwise, it will eventually end on its own, and you have learned something from the experience.

Vital to the task of achieving an independent identity is a knowledge of what kind of sexual people we are. Obviously, an intimate relationship with another person, not necessarily one which involves sexual intercourse, is the most rewarding path to such discovery. But there are times when, for whatever reasons of fear, circumstances, or choice, there will be no one available with whom to express your sexual feelings. During these times, there is nothing wrong with masturbation. In fact, masturbation can be a healthy way to improve your chances for a good relationship with a member of the opposite sex. First, it can reduce the unconscious signals of sexual deprivation you are perhaps sending out (in the form of overeagerness or excessive timidity) which may be getting in the way of meeting the kind of person you are looking for. And second, masturbation is, for women, an excellent means to discover what gives them the greatest pleasure—information which can then be communicated to a partner for a more fulfilling union.

Jack Lee Rosenberg, in *Total Orgasm*, writes, "If you *want* to feel guilty about sex, your attitude toward masturbation is the most popular way to do it. But, if you are through with the eighteenth century and not too interested in self-flagellation, it is worthwhile taking a look at the most positive aspects. . . . The Kinsey reports noted a high frequency of masturbation throughout adult life among people who enjoy other forms of sexual activity as well. Kinsey pointed out that many adults who are not immature in any realistic sense do masturbate, and there is no sense in refusing to recognize this fact. There are reliable statistics to show that masturbatory activity precedes, runs parallel with, and succeeds heterosexual activity in human life, and that it goes on from infancy into very old age. For many people, it is the only form of sexual outlet. . . .

"When no other sexual outlet is available, the advantages of masturbation are obvious, but even when other sexual release is available, masturbation can mean the difference between mediocre or unsatisfactory sexual relations and a full, complete orgastic relationship. . . ."

GOING OUT
AGAIN

Coming to greater awareness of your own and others' individual identities paves the way for a social life with a more varied circle of acquaintances than you might once have thought possible or even enjoyable. When people grant their individuality to themselves and others, they begin to drop the kinds of oppressive need for another person to validate them or give approval to their existence. This often means a radical departure from the past marital relationship. Edna, 40, said, "One reason I have enjoyed going out with so many different kinds of men is that I don't feel that same kind of dependence on what they think of me that I did with my ex-husband. One harsh look from him could wipe me out completely, that's how stifled I was. I felt if he didn't love me all the time, something was wrong with *me*. It's taken time, but now I know that I am a pretty good person, no matter what other people might say. And when I don't fear what others think so much, I'm much more open to many different kinds of people."

In resuming relations with the opposite sex, it is important to recognize the difference between seeing people for themselves and acting out feelings which are really directed toward the past marriage. The spill-overs of those feelings into new relationships can keep us trapped in past patterns. Mark, 34, was consumed with bitterness toward his wife for having walked out on their eleven-year marriage. He said he felt rejected and victimized by what she had done, and told me that for two years after his divorce he operated on the assumption that all women were bitches. "I was determined I was going to get even with the screwing my wife had given me by screwing every woman in San Francisco."

An attractive man with prematurely gray hair who could look alternatively boyish and sophisticated, Mark said he had no trouble conning all sorts of women into bed. "I used to take out three or four different women a week. I was totally cold-blooded about it. I figured out what they wanted me to be and what they wanted to hear and I told them. You know, I love you madly, this is the real thing—anything to get them into the sack. I got so I could always spot their weak points, and I made out nine times out of ten. Sometimes the women were out for the same thing. You'd be surprised at how many women there are like that. A lot of them, though, were looking for something more permanent, and when I could see that starting I cut things off quick. I got a kick out of conning all those women—maybe that's why I did it for two years—but the last six months have been really boring. After a while it's all the same, and I want something more now. When I can't even remember their names the next morning, I figure it must be time to stop."

Mark's experience, from which he learned a great deal about himself, illustrates the difference between open experimentation with one's single identity and the self-defeating repetition of the past. Rejected by his wife, Mark felt hostile toward her and hated himself as a failure. Sex

became the mechanical means by which he tried both to
punish himself and his former wife, and satisfy his need to
feel wanted as a man. Predictably, he attracted a great
many women who were playing just the kind of victim
role he himself was acting out. Whenever he found himself with a woman who wanted to develop the relationship, he backed off fast to avoid getting hurt again. Fortunately for him, his boredom and discontent had become so
overwhelming that by the time he had joined my seminar
he was ready to take a look at why he was behaving as he
was, and try other avenues toward a more fulfilling relationship.

However, even when the past no longer predominates,
many mature divorced men and women reentering the
world of single social life have trouble getting their bear-
ings. They know they are no longer blushing virgins or
randy teen-agers, but most of them have no other frame
of reference to fall back on. Gwenn, 42, said she was torn
between the damaged-goods and the prim-and-proper
images. "I knew it was ridiculous to be outraged at the
suggestion I might be interested in sex. After all, I didn't
have my three children through immaculate conception.
But I didn't know any other way to handle the situation.
Standards are so much looser now than when I was single
before. I was confused at first; every situation seemed to
be either-or. I thought if I took one step off my pedestal I
would fall into the pit of the desperate divorcee."

A creative divorce will build the sense of security you
need to assert your own interests in new social situations.
Nina, 47, said that during the first months of her divorce
she let herself fall into some predicaments she would have
preferred to avoid. "At first, I had a hard time turning a
man down," she said, "just like I could never say no to
my husband. I went on a ten-day cruise to the Caribbean,
and every time I went into the ship's lounge I would be
approached by some creep. And I could never say no—
whether for a drink, or a dance, or whatever. I felt com-

pletely vulnerable. Not any more. When I started thinking about why I was attracting those types, I could see that maybe I was coming on like a loser myself. Now I feel a lot more confident about what *I* want. I must not be radiating the same image any more. I think it must have something to do with the fact that I can control the situation now. If a man asks me to dance, I can dance, if I want to, without worrying about what comes next. If I want to end it there, I can end it. Most men will accept this as part of the game. In fact, I find that men look to women to set the limits and call the shots. Many newly divorced women don't realize at first the power this gives them. I know I didn't."

Some divorced people have indulged in harmless flirtations or even extramarital affairs during their marriages, but when the protective shield of marriage is stripped away, the same behavior takes on new and frightening overtones. As a forty-five-year-old man told one of my seminars, "When I was married, I enjoyed being attentive to women—nothing heavy, you understand, just complimenting them on their hair or dress, or engaging in pleasant chitchat. We both knew that that was all there was to it, but when I first got divorced it changed. I felt that when I paid a woman a compliment I was coming on with her and would have to follow through, perform. It was a scary feeling; I just didn't know if I was up to it, if you know what I mean. At first I avoided women, but one night at a dance I met an interesting woman and I decided, what the hell, I'll play it straight, just be me. If she doesn't like me on that basis, forget it. It worked out fine. She said she liked my honesty. When I took her home I kissed her a few times, but no caveman stuff. We've progressed beyond that point since then. The sex is damned good, but I would never have known if I hadn't leveled with her from the start."

Paradoxically, the same fears of women can produce an opposite approach. Marie, 41, was seriously disturbed when almost every man she met asked her to go to bed during their first conversation. "My initial reaction was to think there must be something about me that made them think I was easy," she said. "A friend of mine told me it just proved all men were only interested in sex. It's true, many men would say, 'I think you're great, let's go over to my place for a drink.' But I have come to believe that this may be the only way some men know to say hello. They're so wrapped up in all that he-man stuff. Now when it happens I don't automatically turn off or get insulted. If I find the man attractive, I may say something like, 'Thanks, but hold on a minute. I like you, but you're going too fast for me; let's just slow down a little.' Most of them accept this, in fact many seem to be relieved. Then we talk, and sometimes get started on a relationship at a different level."

I have known many men who will deliberately come on strong out of an unrecognized desire to be rejected. Roy, 37, said he used to proposition women pretty bluntly, and get turned down just as decisively. "Once at a party I walked up to a woman I had never seen before and told her I'd really like to go to bed with her. You know what she said? She said, 'Okay, why not?' I was so floored I never followed through." The clue to Roy's problem lay in the inappropriate repetitiveness of his approach; it was always the same no matter how often he was turned down. He *wanted* to be rejected, because of his belief that he was a personal failure as a result of his divorce. Like Groucho Marx's quip that he would never want to belong to a club which would have him as a member, Roy believed that no one of any real value would want to associate with a "worthless" person like himself and that if they did, they must be worthless, too.

UNSEEK AND
YOU SHALL FIND

Where can I meet nice, interesting men? Where can I meet nice, interesting women? These are the two most common questions I get from members of my divorce adjustment seminars. Just as common is the response from others, not necessarily more than normally attractive: "What do you mean, meet men (or women)? I meet them everywhere—at work, at parties, in museums, on the elevator." There seems to be a triple conflict here: if men want to meet women, and if women want to meet men—and if some have no trouble at all—then it can't be *only* the lack of opportunity or a bad figure or advanced age or not enough money or "square" morals. There are practical limitations, of course, which cannot be talked away, although they need not foster bitterness. As one woman said, "I want to love and be loved. That's the most important thing for me. But I know that just wanting it won't make it happen. In the meantime, even if I'm not in love, I can act in a loving way. I can be sincerely warm and friendly toward all kinds of people. If I'm genuine, I'm sure somebody nice will pick up my message."

Don, my bartender friend, confirms what students of human behavior have learned about the importance of body language—those nonverbal and unconscious cues we send out—in getting the message across. "I really feel sorry for some of the women I see at parties or receptions. I know they really want to meet someone, and yet there they are, hunched up in a corner or so defensive that they scare people off. And the men, if anything, are worse. If they aren't grouped together discussing ball scores, they're coming on like gangbusters It's a shame, really."

The solution to finding someone new grows out of the very same process of personal growth which in a creative divorce begins with separation. With your awareness of each person's uniqueness, including your own, and in the course of pursuing the development of your own interests and abilities, you will meet people with whom you feel compatible under conditions which will permit a full expression of everything you both have to offer, not just smart cocktail conversation or sexual intercourse. I have found that the men and women in my seminars who have the greatest success meeting nice members of the opposite sex don't really go out looking. They project a feeling of well-being and a sincere liking of people that is attractive to others. In my opinion there are three reasons for their success:

1. *They believe that, when all is said and done, the emotional similarities between men and women far outweigh the differences.* Sometimes I pass around the following list of actual quotes and ask members of my group to decide which were said by men and which by women:

"I was crushed and needed to learn to stand on my own feet."

"Before every date I was so scared I would pace up and down the hall of my apartment. I was petrified of the opposite sex."

"I always wanted to be married because I felt I had no worth except as a married person."

"I was afraid of the opposite sex before I married—and I guess I still am."

"I'm so anxious that I never have any luck with other people. They must sense it, somehow."

"In most new relationships I usually rush in, but then I back off because I get scared."

They are always surprised to learn that all of these statements came from recently divorced men. Many men in the group, who may be harboring the same feelings themselves, still believe that their reactions must be unique to them; and many of the women find it difficult to believe that a man could experience these feelings. But fear and anxiety, mixed with the desire for new relationships, are common to both men and women. Keeping this similarity in mind can help cut through the artificial, culturally ingrained differences which inhibit the kind of getting together both sexes are looking for.

2. *They do not lose sight of the thrust toward personal growth which began even before their divorce.* Obviously, you will not find all the new people you meet attractive, nor will you always achieve instant rapport. But as one man said, "If I go to a party, talk with five women, and only get turned down by four, I consider that a success. I know five more people than I did when I arrived and I have the chance to get to know one of them further."

The point is not to think you have to settle for something that will impede your own growth and happiness. The best example of this determination was supplied by Carolyn, a woman in her thirties who had blossomed during the course of one of my seminars. "I used to have my husband's meals ready at six on the dot. I even cooled the soup to the temperature he liked. One night he came home and plopped down in front of the TV. I brought his dinner in on a tray, and asked him to try the soup. He opened his mouth and I automatically fed him a spoonful. Then he opened his mouth again. He expected me to feed him the whole bowl! I said, 'Jesus Christ! I'm your wife, not your mother!' threw the soup on the rug, and ran out of the room. That was the end of my marriage."

Taking that step was, for Carolyn, mastering the ultimate challenge; nothing since then has been quite so difficult. "I can remember the first time after the separation I went to a party. It was a cocktail party friends in the city were giving for people I didn't know, and I almost didn't go. I made up all sorts of excuses—the parking, the long drive at night, the strange faces I would meet—but in the end I went, and had a very good time. I even met a nice guy who asked me out. Well, I automatically turned him down—I made some weak excuse—but after I got home I started thinking and decided I really did want to go out with him. So I called him up. I figured if I had the guts to end a miserable ten-year marriage, I could certainly follow through with a new man I liked. We went out, had a great time, and have since become very important to each other.

"That whole experience was a little lesson in life for me. I mean, going to the party was hard for me to do, but I did it, and enjoyed myself. That gave me the courage to call up Frank, and that turned out to be the right thing, too. When I first got divorced I thought that the woman who threw the soup on the rug couldn't be the real me, but it was. That wasn't the act of a crazy woman, it was the coming out of a *person* and so was going to the party and so was letting Frank know how I really felt. It's all connected, and after that blow-up it keeps getting easier."

3. *They are aware of the limitations of sexual and social stereotypes.* Gene Marine, the author of a witty and extremely enlightening book called *A Male Guide to Women's Liberation,* was once asked by a man in one of my seminars how his life had changed as a result of what he learned about himself during the research and writing of his book. His answer illustrates the tremendous liberation and expansion which comes with breaking through stereotyped notions of what men and women are: "It's a slow process, but culturally I feel freer as a person, now that I have started to break a mold into which I had no say in being forced. I still like playing Humphrey Bogart—the old ways die hard—but it isn't a necessary part of me now, and I can laugh at it in a way I couldn't before. My relationships with men have improved markedly. I don't show off or compete with other men as much, and consequently I think I can meet other men more openly and be more interested in them as people and even learn something from them.

"My relations with women as *people* have gotten a lot better, too. I won't begin to pretend that I don't react sexually to women, that I don't turn and look at an attractive woman on the street, but I have found that I can become friends with women in a new way. I've had many women friends in the past, but there was inevitably an undercurrent of sexual tension that is not always present now. This wasn't a conscious effort, and it hasn't evaporated completely, but when I began to see women as people, it stopped being the dominating force. Now I can take other aspects of women more seriously and respond to them more fully.

"I meet a lot more interesting people. One gimmick I learned when I was writing the book has now become a habit. When I go to a party and am introduced to a couple—you know, this is Joe Blow and this is his wife—I turn to the wife and say, 'And what do *you* do?' Usually it floors her: she's never considered the possibility that she's anything besides Joe Blow's wife. But I've met fascinating women this way who do all kinds of interesting things. If I had done this five years ago it would have been a form of flirtation, and my signals would have said so clearly. Now it's not and the response is entirely different, from wives *and* their husbands.

"A final goodie is that my sex life is better—freer, not so much role-playing, more open. Sometimes I slip back into the old games; I don't claim to be totally free of my cultural hangups, but in general sex for me is much more exciting than it was before."

4. *They view the unexpected as a promise rather than as a threat.* Although many men and women in my seminars have expressed this reaction in various ways, the one I remember most clearly came in a letter which Florence, 47, wrote to me six months after her seminar was over: "I now look on each day as an adventure, rather than something I want to run away from. Looking back, I think my attitude changed when I decided to go to my twenty-fifth

college reunion. I was getting so damned bored with my own whining and self-pity that I decided to go. I had no idea of meeting a man; I just wanted to see what had happened to the old gang. My friends warned me that they would all be old, fat, dull, and smug, but I said to myself, 'Okay, but what's the alternative? More whining?' So I went and had a perfectly marvelous time. They weren't dull or fat—not most of them, anyway, and it seemed as if every other person I spoke with had been divorced. I met some old classmates I had lost track of, and made plans to get together with the ones who live near me. One of them was a divorced man I remember vaguely from school, and we've been going out fairly regularly since the reunion.

"And to think that the invitation just appeared out of the blue sky! I shudder now to think that I almost didn't go. That taught me a lesson I won't ever forget: I went with an open mind. I was genuinely curious to see my old classmates, and didn't have any ideas in advance of what they would be like. Some were dull as far as I was concerned, but I know other people wouldn't necessarily think so. I didn't have to judge them, only avoid becoming involved with them.

"Tell your seminars that unexpected events can be good as well as bad, if people look at them the right way. And to try a class reunion. It can provide instant revelation."

Of course, what Florence thinks of as instant revelation is really an awareness born of the personal growth that her creative divorce enhanced. Her ability to view uncertainty as necessary to excitement and new adventure stems from a confidence in all the internal resources she has at her command to meet the challenges of the future—not "new" resources, but attributes she had been developing throughout her life which a creative divorce only released and let flourish.

The interval between the day we are born and the day we die consists in large part of uncertainties and unexpected events. To fear the uncertain or the unexpected is to fear life itself. A creative divorce affords the opportunity to end such fears and begin to see uncertainty as alive with promise as well as possible pain. To know that we alone are responsible for the quality of our lives, that we have inner resources we can tap to meet new challenges, that new situations present us with choices, not finalities—this is the kind of knowledge that can dissipate our fright. The certainty and stability we constantly seek lie within us, not in the outside world.

CHAPTER 7

Seeing the Person in the Child

WHAT HAVE I DONE?

I know of no other aspect of divorce that causes more anguish than parents' fears of how it will affect their children, and their uncertainty over what they can do to minimize its impact. Being a parent, as Sigmund Freud once remarked, is an impossible profession under even the best of circumstances; divorce can expand the truth of his statement to unbearable limits. To say that it is normal for children to react to a divorce in unfamiliar and outrageous behavior; to say that in most cases this behavior will be short-lived; to say that the child, like the parent, can profit from the experience—these are true, but in the first months of separation such truths offer little consolation to the parents whose children seem to be pouring salt in the wounds left by their marital dissolution. As a just-separated mother of two grade-school boys said, "They're driving me crazy! Now that their father is gone, they're constantly out of control. They won't go to bed when they're supposed to, they don't eat, they throw tantrums, and they've forgotten everything we've taught them about neatness. Half the time I spend screaming at them, and the other half worrying about what a shrewish mother and an absent father will do to their development."

Because divorced parents have enough real problems to cope with, it is vital that from the outset they rid themselves of some false notions concerning children and the impact on them of divorce and separation. If they can penetrate the thick layer of guilt which clouds their thinking, they will find a number of common-sense precepts—buttressed by a good deal of research—which suggest that children are far better equipped to weather the storm of a marital break-up than many newly divorced parents would believe:

1. *Children are resilient.* It goes without saying that children are enormously influenced by the quality of their family life and the relationship with their parents. However, short of actual neglect and physical abuse, children can survive any family crisis without permanent damage—and grow as human beings in the process—if they can sense some continuity and loving involvement on the part of their parents. Most divorced parents, by breaking up the two-parent household, are remorseful over having robbed their children of this continuity, but in fact the assurance children need is dependent on their perceptions of a secure future. The extent to which the break-up of a household can shake this security will depend significantly on how sincerely a child believes that his parents loved, valued, and cared for him before the separation. Furthermore, every child, like every adult, has his own internal drive toward emotional and physical health and stability which parents can help to reinforce once they understand what is going on. I do not offer this appraisal of a child's capacity to weather crises as an endorsement of "anything goes" parenthood, but rather to caution parents against the kind of disasterizing which prevents them from recognizing their own child-rearing competencies.

2. *The impact of divorce on children is far less severe than the consequences of remaining in an unbroken but*

troubled home. While many parents may agree with this assertion in the abstract, their confidence wavers in the first weeks and months of divorce when they see their own children so upset and unhappy. The agonies of the moment blind them to the potential for future well-being. Dr. J. Louise Despert, child psychiatrist and author of the outstanding book, *Children of Divorce*, found that among all the troubled children she had treated or was consulted about, there were proportionately far fewer children of divorce than are found in the general population. Her conclusion is heartening to the many divorced parents who now wonder if they did the right thing: "It is not divorce, but the emotional situation in the home, with or without divorce, that is the determining factor in the child's adjustment. A child is very disturbed when the relationship between his parents is very disturbed. . . . Divorce [in these circumstances] is not automatically a destructive experience. It may also be a cleansing and healing one, for the child as well as you. Divorce is not the costliest experience for a child. Unhappy marriage without divorce . . . can be far more destructive."

The more I read about family life today, the more I believe the question parents should ask is not "Will divorce harm children?" but "Can children survive the family?" We have little information concerning the numbers of children who grow up in loveless, friction-ridden, but superficially "tranquil" households. However, we do know the kinds of emotional wounds a very bad marriage can inflict on a child, and we are just beginning to grasp the dimensions of child-beating in American families.

3. *With or without divorce, the process of growing up is often stormy.* This would seem to be a truism, yet many divorced men and women are such prisoners of their tunnel vision that they believe all their children's problems are somehow related to the divorce. Granted, divorce can intensify normal development difficulties and throw a

child temporarily off the track, but basically these problems are inherent in the process of growth. Parents who can keep this in mind will be less likely to overreact to every crisis in their child's life.

4. *A two-parent home is not the only emotional structure within which a child can be happy and healthy.* Although, again, this statement appears to be self-evident, I have known many divorced parents—mothers especially—who exhaust themselves trying to preserve exactly the same kind of home life which existed before the divorce. Rhoda, 37, collapsed under the strain. "I was determined that life would go on just as it had been, even though I had to work," she said. "It seemed that we had made the children suffer enough without asking them to change their way of life. So I wore myself out working all day, spending all my evening hours with the kids, and then cleaning the house after they went to bed. I had no time for a life of my own, but it didn't seem fair for them to have to give up their freedom to help around the house, or miss out on the little niceties they had enjoyed when we were married. As a result, I was so tired and irritable all the time I couldn't give them the kind of support and attention they really needed. I was hung up on preserving the externals."

Many divorced parents feel so guilty for denying their children a "real" family that they forget what it was really like. Children know. As Kenny, 10, said to his mother when she told him about the divorce, "Does that mean you and Daddy won't be fighting all the time?" Actually, what most Americans think of as a "real" family is no longer the only—nor, in the opinion of many, the best—structure for raising children. This does not represent a retreat from the family *per se*, only a recognition that the family as we know it may be too fragile to sustain the pressures of modern life. As Margaret Mead has written: "What most Americans think is the American family is really the post-World War II suburban family: totally isolated, desperately autonomous, unable to tolerate adolescent children at home, pushing its children out into matrimony as rapidly as possible, no grandparents, no cousins, no nothing. . . ."

Fortunately for divorced parents, attitudes toward family life and parenthood are changing—if not rapidly, then certainly profoundly. More and more men and women are proving that single-parent families can be happy and supportive places. Never-married mothers are keeping their children and even men and women who have never been married are adopting offspring. New arrangements to spread around the burden (and the joy) of child care—ranging from neighborhood baby-sitting pools, to day-care centers, to part-time work schedules for husband and wife, to communal living—are on the increase. In larger cities there are organizations of single fathers and mothers who exchange information and work together on common problems. Every day brings more articles about fathers happily raising children without benefit of mother, and of mothers for whom the joys of child-rearing are not great enough to offset their need to develop other aspects of their personalities. Although the fact that these departures rate news coverage attests to their still-experimental nature, their growing popularity suggests a future of expanded alternatives to the traditional two-parent family.

5. *The parents who take care of themselves will be best able to take care of their children.* Divorced parents, by using the mourning process to arrive at a new understanding of who they are as independent men and women, can more easily see their children as independent people, too, and can deal with children's problems compassionately and objectively without feeling defensive, rejected, or guilty. Comfortable with their ability to fulfill themselves, they can minister to their children without unconsciously manipulating them. Unlike the divorced father who feels that every dollar he spends for personal pleasure is a dol-

lar denied his children (or the mother who becomes super-mom to atone to her children for the "sin" of having di-vorced), parents who have lived through a creative divorce realize that sacrificing personal growth "for the sake of the children" places an intolerable burden of guilt on their off-spring which inhibits the happiness of all concerned, and stifles an honest and open relationship between parent and child.

CHILDREN MUST
ALSO MOURN

At the outset of a separation or divorce, such a relation-ship seems impossible. Indeed, most parents would settle for an armed truce. First, they want immediate solutions to a whole series of unexpected problems. Why, if divorce is preferable to a destructive family life, should their chil-dren suddenly start to be so difficult? How can they help their children adjust to a new life when they themselves feel so inadequate to the task? What is the proper balance between the honest expression of feelings and the unwar-ranted burdening of young ears with the details of a mar-ital dissolution? What can ever assuage the staggering guilt of having denied their children the stability of a "normal" family? Where does the hope for continuity lie between mother and child, and between father and child, now that the union has been severed and the household broken up?

The answers begin with the understanding that, in their own unique way, children of divorce go through the same process of mourning as their parents do. If you, as par-ents, are to afford them the healing benefits of this pro-cess, you must first acknowledge such feelings as anxiety, guilt, fear, and anger in yourself. Parents often think they can hide "unpleasant" feelings from their children but in fact the emotional antennae of the young are far more sensitive than those of adults. Any attempt on a parent's part to mask real feelings will cause a child to pick up conflicting signals—the truth *and* the coverup—which will only increase his own anxiety. Even the youngest children are extremely sensitive to the emotional state of their parents. As Shirley Luthman writes in *Intimacy: The Essence of Male and Female.*

Infants can handle all kinds of ups and downs ... in a family without any long-lasting ill effects as long as the parents are facing their problems and their feelings and deal directly with themselves and each other about them. During times of extreme crisis in a family ... the infant will normally react with a slower growth flow or even with a regression. For example, he may go back to crawling when he has just started walking. However, he will quickly resume when the crisis is past and often have a growth spurt then. What is really intrusive to his growth is repressed, unresolved feeling in his parents. They may think they are living with their repressed feelings adequately, but such repression produces in them a kind of low-level tension to which the child is acutely attuned. ... He is constantly perceiving two messages at the same time—warmth and tension. As a result, he has to split his energy to deal with his own growth and also with the tension he is receiving.

Parents who through a creative divorce have learned to express their feelings to their children without conflict will be able to perform a vital parental function: to help their offspring exorcise the "divorce demons" running rampant in their youthful minds. For, while children go through the same steps in the mourning process as adults (the separation shock; the denial; the eruption of strong anger, hostility, and guilt; the withdrawal; the gradual testing out of the new reality; and the letting go of the two-parent, single household family relationship) their grasp on external truth is not nearly so strong as the power of their internal fantasies which divorce or separation can conjure up. If allowed to flourish unchecked, they can terrify a child. What he needs are parents who can simultaneously appreciate these hidden feelings and also reassure him that, while perfectly acceptable as feelings, they do not explain the entire truth of the matter.

To appreciate fully the power of these divorce demons, parents need to understand how children view the world around them and their position in it—and by children I mean boys and girls from birth through adolescence. The immaturity of children—their lack of worldly experience, and their emotional and physical dependence on their parents which is total in their early years and still significant into adolescence—renders them vulnerable to massively frightening feelings of abandonment, resentment, hostility, and anger which erupt within them at the time of their parents' divorce or separation. Unmitigated by the confidence that he can take care of himself, these feelings become monstrous realities to a child. He feels actually abandoned, and can become terrified at the prospect. Suddenly one parent is no longer there. If one half of his stable world can so easily disappear, what will prevent the other half from vanishing? Who will be there tomorrow to protect and care for him? According to the logic of childhood, these are perfectly logical fears. At such times a child who was quite self-sufficient before the separation may become extremely fearful of being left alone with a baby-sitter, or will resist going out to play for fear that when he returns his one remaining parent will have left.

To counteract his terrors of abandonment, it is common for the child to deny the reality of his parents' divorce. Many times this denial takes the form of turning into "mama's brave boy" or "little helper," and parents will sigh with relief that their children are "taking it so well." They should look further. A mother of an eleven-year-old boy was initially gratified that her son was mature enough to accept her explanation of the divorce. As the months passed, however, she was puzzled by the seemingly contented, smiling facade he presented. She could detect no outward reaction to his father's absence. When his teachers reported a marked decline in his schoolwork, she took him to the school psychologist. It turned out that, in spite of her repeated statements that the marriage had ended, the boy continued to believe that his mother and father would eventually be reunited. The longer the separation continued, the more the boy was forced into his fantasy life to maintain his desperate hope for reconciliation, and the less energy he had left to devote to school.

Breaking through this barrier requires a parent to be alert to even small signals a child sends out; correctly perceived, they can mean the beginning of an improved parent-child relationship. A mother in one of my seminars reported that she felt her seven-year-old daughter was suffering from the divorce, but she was not able to expose her pain to daylight. One evening they were both looking at the newspaper and came across a photograph of a mother with two children but no father. Her daughter said, "I don't like that picture," and quickly covered it with her hand. The mother, alert to the feeling behind the statement, said, "I know, it hurts very much not to have Daddy here, doesn't it?" With that, the little girl burst into a torrent of tears, and for the first time they were able to talk about what she really felt. This incident was the beginning of a more open and stable relationship between them.

When parents succeed in helping their children to bring feelings to the surface, they must be prepared to deal with the logic of a child's mind. Youthful guilt, for example, is a far more potent guilt than his parents feel in that it comes from the child's magical conviction that he is all-powerful. Children are often unable to distinguish between wish and reality; to them their wishes are deeds. It might seem contradictory to state that children are at the same time totally dependent on adults and yet remain convinced of their own total control, yet it is emotionally true. I know of no child of divorce who has not felt that he or she was somehow responsible for the break-up, even though this belief may never be directly expressed. If a child at some point has wished his mother or father dead or absent (and what child has not?) he may draw the conclusion from the divorce—illogical to adults, but terribly compelling to him—that the actual departure is the direct consequence of his wish.

The very young child may never be able to state this conviction in words; the older boy or girl will often ascribe the divorce to some remembered instance of his or her misbehavior: "If only I hadn't cried at the dinner table, Daddy wouldn't have left," or "Mom and Dad split because I got in trouble at school." As children mature, they begin to relinquish a belief in the magical power of their thoughts to become actions, but a divorce crisis can reactivate, even in adolescents, this childish but powerful notion. Parents who realize this fact can take steps to relieve their children of the burden of illusory wickedness by assuring them that the marital break-up was the decision of two adults, not the product of their children's thoughts, feelings or actions.

Anger, too, is a large component of a child's reaction to the divorce of his parents—anger made stronger by his view of the world as revolving totally around his needs. Indeed, this is the very definition of childish behavior; nothing in a baby's life contradicts it, and well into adolescence a child feels that his parents are there solely for his benefit, because he is so dependent on them for protection and care. It is essential that both parent and child face the expression of anger at the time of separation; otherwise it can fester and grow, and later on become unmanageable—especially when the child sees his mother or father resume a private life in which new attachments to a member of the opposite sex are formed.

For parents who never learned how to handle anger, expressions of anger from their children can be hard to take. Sharon, 32, and the divorced mother of six-year-old Wendy, said that her daughter cried and cried when she and her husband separated. "She kept saying, 'Can't we get Daddy back? You're bad for sending him away. I hate you!' and other really awful things," Sharon remembers. "I just didn't know how to handle her. Whenever anybody came to visit she would interrupt constantly, going on and on like a racehorse—crawling under the dining-room table, jumping on the furniture—really weird behavior. She started school that fall and didn't do well at all. The teachers said she was acting out in class and being very provocative with the little boys.

"I tried to convince myself that this was just a phase, but when it kept on I got scared and called the school counselor, who suggested some family therapy for Wendy and me. Thank God for that, it was the best thing for both of us. One of the most important things I learned was how to handle Wendy's anger. I found out I was scared to death of anger. First my mother and then my husband used angry outbursts to get me to do what they wanted. When Wendy did the same thing, I went to pieces. I'd get very frightened and then very remorseful and would end up begging for her forgiveness.

"Now it's different. First of all, I don't feel I immediately have to make the situation right—there are some things you just can't make right. But I can tell her I know she's angry and that if we can we'll try to do something about it. Actually, it's not what I say so much as it is that I don't fall apart inside when she gets angry. I used to feel the whole world rested on my shoulders and I couldn't let anything go wrong, or let anyone know I wasn't perfect. Now I don't get so upset if things don't go exactly as I planned. I give myself more leeway.

"My change in attitude has made all the difference in my relationship with Wendy. There's none of that tension between us any more. Before, if she had said something to make me angry or upset, like last month when she said she didn't want to go to summer camp, my response would have been 'You *have* to go, a lot of nice kids will be there and you'll like it.' Then Wendy would have gotten angry and I'd feel guilty for provoking her. Now I can listen to what she's telling me *behind* what she's saying, that she's really anxious about going away, and I respond to that feeling. Before I was denying her the right to have any feelings I felt threatened by. This time, I told her that I knew she was upset about going to camp because she was afraid she wouldn't know anybody, and she began talking about her fears. It was a great relief for her to know that I understood, and I was able then to deal with some of what she was afraid of. Incidentally, she did go to camp and had a good time."

When parents establish a climate in which the child feels free to express all his feelings that the shock of separation has triggered—the anger, despair, guilt, anxiety, fear, resentment—they can pinpoint the needs of the child that gave shape to his fantasies. These needs can guide the parents in what they say to reassure their children of continued love, and also what they tell their children about the divorce. Many parents feel children should be spared the facts of a divorce, and indeed there is no reason to get into areas of recrimination and personalities with them. Nevertheless, parents who think that by sweeping the truth under the rug they can fool their children are really fooling themselves. Emotional truth cannot be kept from a child; if you do not supply him with an explanation which is based on truth, he will make one up based on his own fears and fantasies, and you can be certain that it will be far more terrifying to him than what really happened. Children are entitled to an explanation—not long, self-justifying speeches, just an honest explanation that is appropriate to the age and understanding of the child.

So, paradoxically, it is this period of greatest family

uproar, when parents themselves feel most vulnerable and inadequate, which provides the opportunity to lay the groundwork for future emotional stability and family health. It is the child who never shows his feelings, the boy or girl who appears to be the very model of adjustment, who may well bear the permanent emotional scars. This is the time to help your children acknowledge their inner feelings without fear of censure, and to let them know what you are going through. They can then complete the process of mourning by learning to let go of the old family relationship, secure in the knowledge that although their lives have changed, they will have a continuing, stable relationship with both their parents, even though their parents are now living in separate households.

CHILDREN
ARE CHILDREN . . .

There are certain reactions to divorce on the part of children which seem to be tied to the specific stages of their development. Your awareness of these possible reactions may help you cope more effectively with offbeat behavior, and to distinguish those normal but intensified development "crises" from more serious setbacks*:

Infancy. When a divorce occurs during the mother's pregnancy or while the child is very young, the infant will be affected by whatever grief and depression his mother feels, insofar as she is unable to give him the care he needs. He may react by changing his customary patterns of eating, sleeping, and eliminating. He may cry for more holding, rocking, and attention. It is important for the divorced mother not to drown her baby with all the love

---

* For the structure of the following analysis I am indebted to Dr. E. H. Klatskin for her excellent article, "Development Factors," which appears in *Children of Separation and Divorce*.

and attention she once gave her husband. If such attention is too indulgent, the child may become spoiled; if too domineering, he may never achieve self-reliance as an adult. To provide the proper balance of care and autonomy her baby needs, the mother must seek out a life of her own for gratifications a baby should not be expected to provide.

Preschool. A preschool-age child whose parents divorce has usually known the presence of both mother and father; with separation, he must adjust to an actual loss as well as to a break in his daily routine. A common response to children of this age is to regress to earlier forms of behavior: they may temporarily lose the recently gained control of bowels and bladders, eat poorly, have temper tantrums and nightmares. Parents should avoid berating the child for being infantile; such behavior is his way of showing anxiety, fears, and anger he cannot express in words. It is his way of mourning, of taking one step back before he can again take two steps forward. When divorce occurs later during the preschool period, the boy or girl, who has begun to develop strong ties with the parent of the opposite sex, may feel terribly guilty and responsible if the other parent leaves. In the child's mind, the wish for the removal of that parent has come terrifyingly true. For this reason, psychologists believe it is important that the child see the absent parent at frequent intervals during this period, even if only briefly, to help allay his fears that he "wished his parent to death." Many parents are so upset by the stormy aftermath of these visits that they prefer the absent parent to stay absent, so that the child can adjust to this new life without having his grief constantly rekindled. However, as Dr. E. H. Klatskin has found: ". . . in the long run, the results obtained from helping [the child] to accept both the reality of the 'other' parent's absence from the home, as well as his continuing relationship with this parent, would appear to outweigh the short-term disadvantages of a temporary emotional upset." Dr. Klatskin draws the parallel between children of divorce and hospitalized children who, while terribly upset following a parent's visit, nevertheless made a faster emotional recovery upon returning home than did children whose parents were not allowed to visit them in the hospital.

School-age and preteen. As the child moves into the world and comes under the influence of teachers and other children his own age, he will begin to form his own perceptions about life. If divorce occurs during this period, the child will be aware of the existence of emotional problems between his parents which preceded the separation. He needs an explanation from them which will square with the turmoil he has correctly perceived. Parents should be guided in their explanations by the children's questions. Past the age of five, children must be assumed to have many questions, even if they do not ask them. Connie, a thirty-six-year-old mother in one of my seminars, said that before her husband left they both sat down with their two daughters and for three hours tried to explain what was going to happen, that they would both continue to love their children, and that the divorce was not the result of anything either of the girls had done. "It was awful," she recalls. "I cried, John cried, and Susan, the four-year-old cried. But Mary, the seven-year-old, turned cartwheels and played with her doll. She seemed totally oblivious to what we were saying. Later that evening, as I was putting her to bed, I asked her how she really felt and she burst into tears. Then we really talked it out. She said, 'Why did you make Daddy go away?' I told her it was something Daddy and I had decided on together, and I think she felt better then. She asked the same question every once in a while for a few weeks after that, but not any more. Just the same, every two weeks or so I make a point of telling them I know how much they must miss their father. They don't say much, but I think they appreciate knowing I am aware of their feelings."

School is one of the most common areas in which a child of this age will express his anxiety and fears. It is not unusual for very good students to get failing grades under the initial impact of their parents' divorce. Such deterioration in schoolwork may reflect the child's anxiety over his disturbed family relationship, or his desire to punish himself for "causing" the divorce. It may also result from an unrecognized urge to "get even" with his parents for having separated by refusing to "perform" in endeavors that he knows are significant to them. Sometimes a child thinks, unconsciously, that by making things hot for his parents he can bring about their reconciliation. By misbehaving in school he may be saying, in effect, "Look at how much trouble I can cause because you are separated. I'll stop if you get together again."

The hopes of children for a parental reconciliation provide another reason for both spouses to deal with the push-pull aspects of separating as honestly as possible. Overly friendly relations between them can be just as devastating in terms of raising childish hopes as all-out hostility. Connie admitted that during the first weeks of separation John often came over for dinner. "At first I thought it was good for the girls to see that they father and I could still be friendly," she said, "but then I discovered that both girls thought we were in the process of getting back together. Maybe part of me was wishing the same thing, so I decided to call a halt. It was just too painful for everybody. Now they see their father by themselves, and it works out better all the way around."

An older child, who is beginning to separate himself from his parents' views, is especially sensitive to hypocrisy from his mother and father. If he detects insincerity in his parents' relationship, he will often conclude that insincerity is a characteristic of their behavior in other situations as well. This is a period when he is beginning to form close relationships with other children his own age. While in the past a child of divorce was often ostracized by his friends for being "strange," the rising divorce rate, by adding one million children each year to his ranks, guarantees that in most communities the child of divorce can find a measure of support and understanding from his friends. If parents are to keep the lines of communication open to their children, they will have to be as honest with them as possible.

Adolescence. In even the most stable two-parent family, adolescent children can test the limits of parental patience and understanding. Struggling with internal bodily change and the need to carve out an adult identity, the adolescent is unpredictable and ambivalent in his behavior and attitude toward his parents, regardless of whether or not they are divorced. Possessing a certain amount of personal experience, but still dependent on his parents, the adolescent is supermature one moment and childish the next. Dr. Klatskin has pinpointed a divorced parent's tendency to consciously or unconsciously foster one of these two extremes as the greatest danger to the teen-ager's healthy development. Relying on a teen-age child as the "man" or "woman" of the house, or treating a teen-ager of the opposite sex as a "date" is just as harmful to that child as not providing discipline or encouraging dependent behavior for fear of losing the child's love—and presence.

Adolescents need parents as parents—not as boyfriends or girl friends—who can set reasonable limits on their children to protect them from their own frightening impulses, and to show them that they are still loved. One mother of a teen-age girl reported that after the separation her daughter seemed to change overnight from a docile and contented child into a little hoyden. "She would sometimes stay out all night," the mother said. "I thought if I got tough she would run away from home. But after one ferocious argument I really laid down the law; strangely enough, she seemed to calm down a little." There was really nothing strange in this behavior. The girl was testing her mother's concern, which the mother indicated by being firm. What the mother had seen as providing freedom, the daughter had interpreted as lack of interest.

For adolescents, a parent's remarriage or resumption of serious dating may prove more disruptive than the divorce itself, since a teen-ager can usually appreciate the strains in his parents' marriage and comprehend the explanation they give him for the divorce. He or she may be less able to handle the hidden sexual and competitive jealousies the presence of a stepparent (or a close "friend") can arouse. Children find it hard to accept the fact that their parents are people in their own right and that such "old people" need and want affection and love from a member of the opposite sex in a relationship which excludes the children. Your attention or love for another person may seem to the teen-ager as the withdrawal of your love and attention from himself. He may express his anger and anxiety by resisting discipline, becoming delinquent, failing school courses, or coldly ignoring you and your friends.

Open communication based on feelings can minimize these and other reactions of your children, and guarantee that they will be transitory. In the long run, however, one of a parent's most useful resources is the memory of his or her own adolescence. Remembering the intense ambiguities of our own youth can help us empathize with (if not condone) all the wild behavioral swings of our adolescent children. Anxiety, vulnerability, and insecurity are built in to the process of growing up, whether or not we have lived in a one- or two-parent home. The memory of the growing pains you went through to separate yourself from your parents can increase your understanding of the dilemmas of your own children.

... BUT CHILDREN
ARE PEOPLE, TOO

Although knowing a certain reaction to be typical to children of a particular age can help, the fullest and most satisfying relationship with your children is born when you begin to see them as separate people as well as your own flesh and blood. In marriages heading for divorce both parents are often so wrapped up in their own concerns that they have no time or energy to really look at (and listen to) their children. Yet, inside each of our sons and daughters a person is struggling to emerge and be recognized. Out of the shared experience of mourning in a creative divorce can evolve a close relationship between two people based on their acceptance of each other for what they are rather than what they "must" be.

Taking a really good look at our children as people rather than as extensions of ourselves and our needs is admittedly difficult, because our children *are* extensions of ourselves, genetically speaking. Yet in many ways we continually transgress the invisible boundary between us and them, playing on the biological connection to the detriment of their individuality. "I believe that if it were not for the intrusion by the parents, most children would be obviously unique and very unlike either parent," writes Shirley Luthman in *Intimacy: The Essence of Male and Female.* "I think that what is actually inherited is minuscule. It would be the exception rather than the rule that any child would resemble his parents in personality [were it not for parental intrusion]." Mrs. Luthman's catalog of unwitting intrusion by parents runs the gamut from the apparently trivial to the profound:

- taking physical liberties with children—picking them up suddenly, grabbing their hands, arbitrarily moving them from one place to another, or simply holding them when they do not want to be held

- assuming that a young child does not know what he thinks or feels
- interrupting children without apology or explanation
- failing to consider a child's feelings when making decisions affecting him
- superimposing male and female stereotypes on children's behavior
- attempting to control what a child feels by labeling his feelings "good," "bad," "appropriate," or "inappropriate"

Clearly every child—from birth through adolescence—needs parental help in establishing limits so that he does not intrude on others. But equally as important is the child's need to make his own choices on the basis of who he is and how he feels. When we deny children respect for their own feelings we are infringing on their dignity, saying, in effect, "You aren't good because you aren't like me, or because you don't do what I tell you to do." Letting a child be himself does not require abdication of parental responsibility. As Mrs. Luthman explains, "[A child] can tolerate changing his behavior to suit you if you, as the parent, recognize that he has the right to feel differently than you do without a loss to his self-esteem. . . . He can act on his feelings and feel free to express himself, knowing that he will get 'sat on' at times but never belittled, cut down, or lessened. . . . [He] grows into an adult who is clear and secure in the knowledge that he is most effective by being himself. He can survive and get what he needs without sham, pretense, manipulation, or distortion. That knowledge is the basis of the individual's sense of himself as a whole, autonomous person."

GAMES
NOBODY WINS

Parent and child are not natural enemies, yet when neither has a clear picture of the other (or of himself) as a separate, autonomous person each can unwittingly become enemies to the other's self-esteem. A divorce crisis can intensify these mutually victimizing games—parent against child, child against parent, parent against parent through the child—precisely because all concerned are so dependent on each other for emotional stability. When the divorce destroys the daily routine and accustomed roles which once provided this stability, both parent and child— if they are unable to find security by sharing their feelings openly—can fall into some destructive game-playing to reestablish a sense of control and permanence.

One of the most common games parents play with their children is *At Least We've Got Each Other,* in which the mother or father tries to fill the need for adult love and companionship with his or her children. It is one thing for a child to assume some of the legitimate housekeeping functions that a mother or father once performed; it is quite another to require that child to satisfy needs only another adult can supply. Mothers telling their sons, "You're the man of the house now that Dad isn't here," or fathers who "date" their teenage daughters with flowers, restaurants, and nights on the town place their children in an intolerable situation: are they children or adults, boys and girls or lovers, cared-for or caretaker?

Out of similar unfulfilled needs arises *Pals.* Suddenly Dad tries to lose twenty pounds, lets his hair grow long, dresses in clothes fifteen years too young for him, and begins talking teen-age slang to his son. Mother dons a micro-miniskirt, tells her daughter "just think of me as your older sister," competes for the attention of her daughter's friends, and insists on unburdening intimate details of her social life. This is not mother-daughter sharing, but mother's attempt at trying to recapture a bit of youth. As one adolescent girl complained, "Friends are people my own age and I can find them anywhere. But I only have one mother, and suddenly she's turned into a forty-five-year-old teen-ager."

Nothing's Too Good For My Child is a direct outgrowth of unresolved feelings of guilt in mother or father. These parents drown their children in excessive care and attention in an effort to assuage their feelings that they have done a terrible thing to their children by divorcing. A father up to his ears in debt who shells out for a new car for his son, saying "I owe it to him," is playing this game, as is the mother who wears her threadbare coat for another winter so that her daughter can buy that new dress she simply must have. Indulgence of children's whims constitutes the rule of this game, which has as its unrecognized conclusion the child's loss of respect for the parent, and a perpetuation of infantile behavior.

Poor Little Me gets started when a parent, unable to accept responsibility for controlling his or her life, uses the guise of being "open" with the children to elicit their pity and support. "Thank God you're still here, how could I ever survive without you" may be intended as praise, but it puts a heavy burden on a child, who is not equipped to respond. Parents should not fear admitting vulnerability and uncertainty to their children—deliver us from supermoms and superdads!—but to imply that you are so helpless that you can no longer play your proper role as parent is demoralizing to your children, and to your own self-esteem.

When either parent is still emotionally embroiled in the past marriage, he or she can dream up an endless variety of *Getting Even* games in which the children become the vehicles for revenge. *Over My Dead Body*, while camouflaged with a lot of verbiage about the child's best interests, is basically a game of custody and visitation rights in which one spouse seeks to inflict pain on the other by denying the opportunity to see or have the children. In its mildest forms, Over My Dead Body means not notifying Daddy about a child's last-minute vacation changes, or the sudden discovery of an "illness" which will prevent the child from visiting his father. It also includes bringing the children back late from a weekend with father, or not showing up to take the children in full knowledge that ex-wife will have to cancel plans she has made. When both parents take the gloves off, Over My Dead Body can entail moving to another state (or another country) so the visiting parent can no longer see the children, and even drawn-out legal battles to have the other parent declared unfit as a mother or father.

Daddy? You Mean That Bastard? is a particularly vindictive spin-off of Getting Even, calling upon whichever parent has the children to vilify the absent parent in front of the children at every opportunity. Parents play the game by convincing themselves that "it's better to be honest with children," but the children, desperate to love both parents, are ping-pong balls in the game of charge and countercharge. As the game goes on, their confusion, helplessness, and anxiety mount.

You Spy is divorce espionage in which the children are the double agents. Sometimes the cover is polite curiosity: "Did you have a good time with your father this weekend? Did you meet any of his new friends?" Sometimes it's a question of asking the children to serve as war-zone messengers: "Here's the child-support check. Give it to your mother and tell her I hope she's happy now that I don't have enough to live on," or "Tell your father when you see him tomorrow that unless he pays the alimony on time, tomorrow will be your last visit with him."

Against such parental onslaughts, children develop

games of their own to reestablish some semblance of security, all of which fall under the general heading *Help!* Feeling that they are objects for their parents to win or lose, sensing themselves used rather than loved, they devise their own methods to gain assurance that they will not be thrown to the wolves. Behind all their games is the unspoken plea, "I want you to know how I feel so that you will stop doing things that are making me so anxious and afraid. Show me that I am all right and that you love me."

Divorced parents, trapped in their own despair, often take their children up on these games without knowing it. All they can see is a once-peaceful child suddenly turned obstreperous monster. The most effective game is *Gotcha!* Like other games, the details of Gotcha! differ according to the methods of dealing with parents that children used during the marriage, and the particular weaknesses of whatever parent they are playing with. A boy who knows his mother is proud of a clean house will turn his room into a pigsty. A girl aware of her mother's concern for what the neighbors think will carry on an argument at the top of her lungs. A son will flaunt long hair and bare feet in his conservative father's face. Whatever the rules, the game is "won" when the parent pays attention to the child.

But Daddy Said I Could is a preferred game for children of divorce, since they generally see only one parent at a time, and can elaborate upon the old divide-and-conquer routine that they played during the marriage. Children who play this game have no sense that their parents really love them, and so desperately seek for some external sign—a gift, a special treat, a waived rule—to provide reassurance. They are adept at manipulating their parents to get what they want: "I don't want to live with you any more, you don't let me stay up late like Daddy does." Obviously a child playing But Daddy Said I Could stands the greatest chance of "success" if his parent is playing Nothing's Too Good for My Child.

Children's games, like parent's games, spring from the need to survive emotionally, although children—unlike their parents—suffer the additional fear that they may no longer be able to survive physically, either. When they play games like these, it means that their basic trust in their parents' ability to love and care for them has been undermined, and that they can only get the love and care they want through manipulations. In the absence of more open and stable family relationships based on shared feelings, the children yearn for a return to their old world where, for better or worse, mother and father lived together and the children knew what to expect, even if their expectations were often unsatisfying. It is that yearning which finds its expression in "impossible" behavior. That yearning—and that behavior—will diminish when their parents start radiating competence and security in their new lives. In a creative divorce some of these games may still turn up, but as side events, not center-stage attractions. As parents become more and more aware of their own feelings and their children's real needs, games of manipulation will yield to healthy and open communication.

CHILDREN AND
LEGAL SETTLEMENTS

Lawyers' offices and the divorce courts are traditional battlegrounds on which many embittered, soon-to-be-divorced parents aim emotional gunfire at each other and end up wounding their children as well. In the heat of their battles they lose sight of the fact that the purpose of a divorce settlement is to resolve equitably the issues of marital property, custody and visitation rights, and spousal and child support. Instead of thinking about their children's welfare, they use the court as a forum for playing the Getting Even game. The consequences of their unacknowledged need to fight the old marriage battles in the divorce proceedings will crop up in their children's anxiety-ridden behavior.

In order to achieve a creative divorce, it is imperative that legal arrangements be worked out that all parties can live with. The alternatives are the cultivation of deep-seated resentment and continued legal battles in an effort to retaliate for losing out in the initial settlement. The emotional fallout will escalate the tension of the children to impossible levels. How divorcing parents view the legalities of the divorce will therefore determine to a considerable extent the kind of ongoing relationship each will have with the children after the divorce.

Ann Diamond, one of the country's outstanding divorce lawyers with a practice in Marin County, California, lays down three guidelines for an equitable divorce settlement:

- Custody and visitation determined in accordance with the needs of the children, rather than those of the parents
- Spousal and child support established in consideration of the needs of the whole family, and adequate to provide for a standard of living not too different from that of the other parent (At the same time it should allow the nonworking wife to obtain training for an appropriate occupation without depriving the husband of the incentive to continue his employment.)
- An equitable division of marital property, with both parties fully aware of the nature and value of their assets and liabilities

Ms. Diamond has found that the emotional overlay of almost every divorce can get in the way of achieving this kind of settlement: "There is a general assumption by the public, as well as by many lawyers, that the two parties to a divorce are equally capable of coming to an agreement that is fair and equitable to each. In my experience this is not the case. Seldom are both parties ready to terminate their marriage simultaneously. Usually there is one party who wants to leave and one who is left and consequently feels rejected. There are great variations in intensity of the emotional problems that men and women face when rejected by their former mates, depending on their general emotional balance, mental health, age, and other factors. Accordingly, their ability to handle the consequences of a marital breakup varies greatly."

The most common emotional problems which inhibit a fair divorce settlement, according to Ms. Diamond, are:

- A rejected spouse, unable to accept the finality of the separation, may agree to almost any demand of the other party in the hope that it will facilitate a reconciliation.
- A woman accustomed to having her husband make all important decisions will continue to look to him for advice, even though he has left her and is no longer interested in protecting her.
- The long-suffering, passive mate often seeks redress in the settlement for all past miseries of the relationship, whether self-inflicted or otherwise.
- When the break-up is sudden, the rejected spouse may be so traumatized that he, or more frequently she, is unable to make any realistic estimate of future financial need.
- The spouse who wants out may feel so guilty that he or she will try to compensate by being overly generous in property division and agree to pay or receive support payments which are too high or too low. The subsequent resentment which can erupt in the long run will only cause further problems for both.

- Because the rejected partner may be too depressed to face any additional pressure, he or she will consent to any financial settlement just to get matters over with.
- One spouse may use the children as a means to punish and get even with the rejecting partner.

If two parents accept the guidelines for an equitable settlement which Ms. Diamond recommends, they can then make a conscious effort to eliminate the emotional overlays that interfere with the legal negotiations. That effort, although difficult, will prove worthwhile, for unless the legal settlement fairly meets the needs of the children and both parents, the quality of the lives of all concerned may well be impaired for years to come.

FATHERS AND CHILDREN: REDISCOVERING EACH OTHER

When divorce hits them, many fathers are surprised and overwhelmed to discover how poignantly they miss their children and the accustomed routines of past family life. I have seen men who once took their families for granted break down and cry when ex-wives obstruct their visiting rights or tell the children to hang up when Daddy calls. Theirs is an honest expression of loss and emptiness. When they realize that their children are no longer part of their daily lives, the great stone faces they are supposed to be crack under the impact, and the emotions that were always a part of them leak out: love, concern, tenderness, gentleness, and affection. When they are separated from their children and forced to acknowledge these feelings, they are often frightened by their intensity, especially if they hold the view that these feelings are "feminine." They may have been unacknowledged in the past efforts to fight marital battles or provide a good living for the family. In a creative divorce they come to the surface, not as "masculine" or "feminine," but simply human. Freely accepted, they become the basis for more satisfying relationships between fathers and children.

The plight of the divorced father is one aspect of the divorce crisis which has received little direct attention. To many ex-wives, he is the "lucky" partner, free from the daily responsibilities of child care, having only to send the monthly check and show up on time to pick up the children. To most of society, he is still the second parent—required to prove that he is a responsible father, but not expected to mind too much being separated from his children. Given these views, it is not surprising that many fathers quell their real feelings and settle for being footers of the bills, weekend baby-sitters, off-stage parents wheeled in only for crises, holidays, graduations, and weddings. Frightened by the enormous sense of loss, the presence of unsuspected feelings of love and tenderness, and a wracking guilt, fathers may lean on the practical limitations of single life as excuses for not being the kind of fathers they would really like to be.

And limitations there are, as Tom, 38, reported. "What can I do with two kids in a one-room apartment? We tried that two weeks this summer, but it didn't seem to work out, so we went places all the time. I can see myself turning into a good-time Charlie with them, but there just doesn't seem to be any other way. Besides, the older boy has a life of his own—Little League, neighborhood friends, scouting activities—and I can't help feeling guilty for taking him away from that. It's getting harder and harder to coordinate my work with their schedules. We just seem to be growing apart. I guess it's inevitable."

Yet, more and more fathers are finding that growing apart from their children is not inevitable. In the first place, more fathers are seeking, and being awarded, custody of their children. While ninety-five percent of all custody cases award children to the mother, there is a growing awareness in the courts that many men are frequently more competent and sensitive parents than their former wives. "The best interest of the child" is increasingly interpreted by the courts to mean that fathers as well as mothers may have custody of the offspring. Today, there are approximately seven million single-parent families in this country, of which nearly twenty percent are headed by men. Every sign points to a growth in this proportion in the future.

Of course, the fact that one parent has custody of the children does not guarantee a close relationship. It is the quality, not the quantity, of time spent together that counts, as many fathers who see their children only on weekends have discovered. Tim, a twenty-seven-year-old teacher, said, "I'm a better father today than I was a year ago when I was married. Sure, I only see the kids on weekends, but now I pay attention to them. I listen to what they say and feel. As a matter of fact, I didn't spend all that much time with them when I was home. Usually all I wanted to do was watch football on television: my body was home but my mind was elsewhere. Now we talk a lot more, and for the first time we're getting to know each other."

Walter, 41, said that when he and his wife separated he felt at first that he had lost "control" over his son. "I always thought of him as just the kind of son every father would want: tall, athletic, good in school, popular with the girls. I was very proud of him for his achievements. But you know, the less I play the proud-father role with him, the more I can see in him as a person. He's really a very sensitive kid, and we've started talking about personal things—like the divorce, for instance—we never would have mentioned before. We enjoy each other's company now more than we did in the past. He notices the change in me, too. He says he feels more relaxed around me now, that I used to like him only for what he did, not what he was."

A new relationship between father and children often begins when the father sees that his frantic search for "something to do with the kids" is not bringing him closer to them. Gary, 36, and the father of a boy, 11, and a girl, 9, turned off the Disneyland Daddy routine partly out of financial necessity, and found the alternative much more rewarding. "It wasn't just the money, although God knows it cost enough to entertain two children all weekend. But after six months of movies, ball games, and restaurants I could see that they were cranky and bored all the time. As a matter of fact Todd complained one Saturday about *having* to go to the movies again. So the next weekend we just cooled it. The three of us went to the laundromat, ran errands, and made dinner together. Jenny actually said she had been worried because she didn't think I could cook for myself. We had a great time, and that's become the routine now: Saturday at home as usual, Sunday maybe out somewhere, or I invite some relatives over—along with a few friends—for a casual meal. Both kids love to help in the kitchen, and I've fixed up the back room as a shop so that we can all putter around. Todd's getting to be a pretty good carpenter, and so is Jenny, but basically what I've tried to do is make visiting me more like being at home than going on a vacation."

Perhaps most surprising to parents of adolescent children is the improvement in relations which a divorce can bring about when it is accompanied by the honest expressions of everyone's feelings. Arnold, 43, admitted, "During the marriage I thought my relationship with my daughter Linda was fine, since God knows I was always at home when I wasn't working. But it's only been since we really talked about the divorce that Linda told me she always felt I was ignoring her, as if I were a million miles away and just didn't give a damn about her. That was a real shocker! I just assumed that she knew how much I loved her without my having to say so. It just goes to show you how much people can misunderstand each other when they don't open up. Now we check out how the other is feeling, and you better believe she gets all my attention now when I see her. The short times each week we spend together since the divorce are much more rewarding than all those years of 'togetherness' when we never really communicated."

Among all the parents and children I have known who used divorce as the start of better relations with each other, David's story is one of the most moving. David is a young friend of mine who was sixteen when his parents' marriage broke up. I remember him then as a rebellious and unhappy teen-ager, experimenting with drugs, and in and out of trouble at school. Now twenty-one and a senior in college, he has pretty much straightened himself out, has gotten out of the drug scene, and is on very good terms with both his parents. I asked him how he thought the divorce had affected his family:

"I knew there was a lot of unhappiness between my mother and father when I was a sophomore in high school," David remembers, "so I suppose I must have known at least a year before that they were going to get a divorce, but I didn't want to face it. They had a lot of really bad fights, but I just couldn't imagine that they would ever split up. My mother would get superemotional and my father would crawl into his shell every time there was a problem. It seemed as if I was always arguing with both of them—mostly about drugs. I don't think the drug thing was related to them; everybody at school was into it, grass mostly, and it just seemed easier to go along. Anyway, I had zero communication with my parents then—lots of words, but we never got through to each other.

"It sounds funny to say, but I think the divorce was a really good thing for all of us. It gave my parents a chance to grow, especially my father. Right after the divorce he went back to school and got a master's degree in journalism and now he's really into something which is incredibly satisfying to him. He's thrown off twenty years of the crap of being a businessman, and he's really happy. So is Mom. It's been harder for her, I think, because she's a woman—but she's looking good, travels a lot, and is starting to go out again. I've got a fantastic relationship with both of them now, especially my father. He's much freer than he used to be and doesn't get hung up on little things or hide behind his shell like he used to. It almost feels strange to have that good a relationship with him now, considering how we used to fight all the time. Neither of them understood me."

Something David said made me think his attitudes, too, had changed as a result of the divorce at least as much as his parents'. "When they first separated, I was away for the summer, and would write them both the same letter, and ask one to pass it on to the other. But then I thought that was a bad idea, so I started writing separately. When I got back home, I lived with my mother until I went to college, but I made a conscious effort to communicate with them separately as two different people. Before the divorce this was a problem I didn't have. They were just my parents, "there." I had never really thought of them as separate people, but I had to when they got divorced. First I did it just to avoid getting caught in the middle. Like, sometimes they would try to use me. My mom felt uncomfortable about calling Dad because she thought a girl friend might be there, so she would ask me to call. I did it for her a couple of times, but then I decided it was her problem and she should work it out.

"After a while, treating them separately just seemed sort of right. They were becoming different people from the mother and father I thought I had known. My father, especially. At first I thought he had really changed, but now I think he probably is just letting himself be the kind of person he always was, but felt he never could be when he was married to my mother. That's probably a marriage that never should have happened. At least, everyone is a lot more open and responsive to his own feelings now, and they both say they feel good to be out of that situation.

"The whole thing has taught me a lesson about marriage. You've got to get problems out in the open when they're fresh and deal with them on the spot. I don't think I'm down on marriage as a result of my parents' divorce, but I don't see it as the only answer, either. I believe that marriage is not the type of thing that has to happen immediately. I'd be very cautious and try to learn a lot about the woman I was going with before jumping into matrimony. I'm all for living together first.

"But if I did get into a marriage and it was going bad and we had to get a divorce, sure it would be very hard but I would try to look at it as more of a positive thing. I don't mean I wouldn't hesitate, but I would look at divorce as something that could help both of us more than our marriage could. I mean, it was hell for my family, but look where we came out."

CONNECTING WITH
YOUR CHILDREN

Although there is no single set of instant solutions to the multiple problems freshly singled parents and their equally beleaguered offspring face, the single most helpful suggestion is to recognize that you and your children are separate, interdependent individuals. If you have successfully emerged from the mourning process with a growing sense of your own autonomy, you can more easily grant your children the same prerogative. When you are more secure in knowing who you are, you can see your children as persons rather than as reflections of your anxieties and frustrations. When children sense that they are seen, loved, cared for, and respected as people, they will respond.

This is not an overnight process. If the divorce represents only a temporary fracture in a warm and loving parent-child bond, the child's emotional disarray will be short-lived. If the past relationship was marred by excessive manipulation by either parent or child, it may take longer to change, but it can happen. Divorce is no excuse for hardening hostility and unease between parent and child; in fact, it can be the opportunity for improved relations. "We grow through adversity. We need not seek it out; whether divorced or not, we can all look back at moments when our lives were in utter chaos, desolation, and despair. Growth comes when we respond to adversity by stretching just an edge beyond our talent and experience. Growth is the result of the stretch. Happiness is the result of the striving."

These are the words of Dr. Robert D. Wald, eminent child psychiatrist and faculty member of the University of California School of Medicine in San Francisco. His guidelines for parents, outlined below, suggest how this growth can improve relations between parents and children of divorce.

Understand what your children want from you. Children want certainty and openness—certainty to experience the world to the best of their ability, knowing that they have their parents' love and support to return to. Children want to be able to count on their parents, so that when they move away from the safety of the home (literally or figuratively) they know it will be there when they return. They want the certainty of being attached to their parents with loosening strings which they themselves can break when they are ready. When they find they cannot, or ought not to have, counted on their parents, they become restless, angry, hurt, disbelieving, and distrusting—all the feelings which are evoked by a sense of betrayal and loss.

And children want openness, an atmosphere in which they can respond to their parents out of the entire array of their feelings, "good" and "bad," and not just those which they have been taught to believe are acceptable. If they can respond to their parents only in certain ways, they may never be able to express the anger and disappointment that the divorce has caused. They may fear that expressing negative feelings will destroy whatever emotional stability they have left in their lives.

Encourage your children to express all their feelings without fear of inhibition, ridicule, or punishment. Make it clear that, while your child may be punished for something he does, he will never be punished for what he says or feels. Recognize that the expression of feelings may be uncomfortable for parent and child. A parent risks being tremendously hurt at hearing what his child thinks of him. If you have trouble listening to the roughened feelings of your child, turn to someone who can help you with your own feelings. Avoid retaliation. The more your child is able to express his real feelings, the less he will express these feelings indirectly through actions. Substitutive actions never provide as much gratification as the simple expression of how he feels, and can lead to real trouble. For example, a fourteen-year-old girl, inhibited from telling her mother the anger and rejection she feels over the divorce, may become disobedient. The mother, unaware of this behavior until the night her daughter doesn't come home until four o'clock, anxiously rushes her to the gynecologist for a vaginal examination. Thereafter, she patrols her daughter like a policeman. The child responds with further defiance, thereby guaranteeing more attention from the mother, who becomes increasingly frantic and repressive. At this point they become locked into a destructive pattern: the daughter gains the desired attention of her mother, but at the cost of her grades, personal autonomy, self-regard, and a peaceful home life. Prevented from talking with her mother about her fear that father has rejected her, she acts out this fear by finding a boyfriend to prove she is loved. But because she is really searching for an answer to the unspoken question concerning her father's

love, that boyfriend won't satisfy her. So she will find another and another until she develops the reputation for
being promiscuous.

If she had been free to express her intitial feelings, she
would be able to modify her behavior in socially acceptable ways. If the mother could say to her daughter, "I
know you're upset and are reaching out for something
you're not getting at home," without feeling defensive, she
might be able to plan activities or just time together with
her daughter to show her interest in their relationship. She
could let her daughter know mother is no goddess, and
that they can both learn together. This paves the way for
the mother to enjoy her child as she is, and to respond to
her child's requests for help.

Appreciate the power of your child's mixed feelings.
The child may need most help in expressing anger and
hostility. Too often when there has been a fracture between parents, the child has learned, directly or indirectly,
that there are "good" and there are "bad" ways to feel.
Typically, love is good, hate is bad, happy is good, sad is
bad. Children raised under these conditions fear their feelings of hatred. They can believe that by expressing "bad"
feelings, they are being disloyal or falling into personal
danger. If, for example, they view divorce as a consequence of expressing torrential negative feelings, they
might be afraid to express their own anger on the chance
that they might be the next ones to be booted out.

If the honest expression of feelings represents a departure from past custom, you may have to sit down with
your child and explain new ground rules, including the
difference between feelings and actions. Authorize the
child to be free to say anything in any voice at the appropriate time and place, but let him know that he will be
held accountable for what he does. He may not *want* to
do the dishes but he doesn't have to, he just has to *do*
them, whether he hates you or not. The recently divorced
mother who can hear her daughter say, "You're bad, you

threw Daddy out, I hate you!" without retaliating will get much more cooperation and respect from the child than the mother who says, "If that's the way you feel about it, go to your room," or "Go live with your father." It may require all her effort to say, "I know you feel that way, but I want you to know I love you very much and no matter how you feel I will continue to be your mother." But the daughter will eventually respond to her mother's reassurance of continued love and care. Because the daughter has been able to express her feelings openly, she will not be forced to express them indirectly through unacceptable behavior.

Results will not be automatic. Since few of us have taught our children to be honestly expressive of the entire range of feelings, some acting out will continue to occur. But if you can accept it as such and continue to invite feelings to emerge, the acting out will diminish. It is only when you get locked in to responding to actions which express feelings indirectly, as in the case of the mother and her "promiscuous" daughter, that the opportunity for expressing feelings directly is lost.

Distinguish between abrupt changes in attitude or behavior reflecting your child's reaction to the divorce and those vicissitudes normal to his development. Normal child development is a bumpy but upward road which defies orderly or precise definition. When the home is not intact, parents are prone to read *divorce* into every normal developmental problem a child goes through. If every time a teen-ager complains about not knowing enough or not being enough the single parent assumes responsibility for wrecking that child's life, the parent will get a warped perspective on just how great his influence as a parent is. Fortunately for parents, the child's natural growth process protects him from many of the mistakes we make; a child's maturation is an intrinsic process and proceeds whether or not we grasp each and every opportunity to help. At the same time, parents newly divorced should be alert to changes in their children's behavior. Any clear and distinct change is evidence that feelings are possibly being expressed indirectly through actions rather than with words. This is the signal to sit down and build an atmosphere in which feelings will emerge. The greater the willingness of the parent to deal with whatever feelings are likely to come forth, the less these feelings will get acted out in discordant and destructive behavior.

As parents you grow and learn about your children at every age. Parents in a creative divorce have learned what it means to live creatively in the present. They have a unique opportunity to live creatively in the present by trying new ways of dealing with their children. Many new events and elements enter a parent-child relationship following a divorce—daily routines, schedules for visits, new feelings—which parents can seize on as handles for a new relationship. If a parent can act on these changes, be they in the home, the time he and the children spend together, the changes in financial status, he can perceive his relationship with his children much as he perceives tomorrow: offering the potential for new and unique solutions rather than guaranteeing repetition of the old and familiar. When parents can anticipate tomorrow based on the fresh experiences tomorrow will include, they are stretching and therefore growing.

Every wheat crop provides the farmer with an opportunity to learn more about growing wheat. If he feels he has to grow it the way he did last year, or the way his grandfather did, he is fixed in the past. As a first-born eight-year-old daughter said to her father, "What do you know about eight-year-olds, you've never had one before!" She knows the truth, but she should also know that no matter how many eight-year-olds her father has, he would never "know about them," because each child—like each day—is new. If we can continue to look at our relations with our children as offering the chance to try new ways of being with them, we will guarantee new experiences with different outcomes from the past. And that is personal growth.

Clearly, these suggestions will not smooth over all the problems between parent and child. But they can result in more cooperation and respect, more regard for differences as well as similarities, more opportunity for children to grow into the unique individuals they are capable of becoming. The process of seeing children as separate people, paradoxically, opens the door to intimacy, that state in which two people continue to grow and change in full awareness of the risks inherent in being open, the state of knowing with a constant certainty that the risks are worth the rewards of increased directness and growing closeness with the other person.

CHAPTER 8

New Commitments

WAS MY DIVORCE CREATIVE?

How can you tell when your divorce has been creative? What is the dividing line between adjusting and growing, between "getting over" and "learning from" the past, between recognizing self-defeating habits and replacing them with more appropriate behavior? These are questions each person must answer for himself, in the light of his past background, present circumstances, and future expectations. Since a creative divorce is a process over time, the answers will arise from the living of your life: your actions will define the quality of your divorce experience. A creative divorce is essentially the beginning of a journey of self-discovery and development, triggered by the crisis of separation, that can go on for as long as you live. The elements of a creative divorce are found in even the earliest stages of separation when you recognize and appreciate the "seeds beneath the snow," those early signs of the undiscovered person that was buried in your marriage. The heart of the creative divorce lies in the process of mourning and how you use it to identify, understand, and "own" the feelings that boiled to the surface during the process. If during the mourning process you were able to get in touch with your feelings and from them build a secure, single-person identity, you set the stage for a reevaluation of every part of your life: your moral and ethical standards, your occupational goals, relations with your children and friends, and your style of life. The degree of actual change you observe will depend on the particular circumstances in your life that you feel needlessly inhibit personal growth, and your willingness to take the risks that being alive—or living creatively in the present—entails. The more you take tiny risks, and see these risks pay off, the more you are moving toward the present. As your self-esteem rises, you become increasingly secure in letting feelings and abilities guide your actions. Each successful act moves you a step beyond the half-person you may have felt, toward the whole person you are becoming. Life then unfolds as a series of challenges you move into with confidence, not confidence that you will always master these tests or that external circumstances will never thwart you, but the confidence of knowing that the only way life can be lived fully and happily is through a commitment to lifelong stretching and growing.

One of the best indications of such a commitment is your willingness to risk new relationships with the opposite sex, relationships with the potential for providing long-lasting closeness and growing intimacy. Your ability to sustain a relationship of this kind without sacrificing your personhood is one of the most tangible signs that you have made your divorce a creative one. There resides deep within every person the need for a relationship with someone else bounded by love, sensual and sexual pleasure, friendship, sharing, warmth, and tenderness—the coming together, in the words of Ford Maddox Ford, for the renewal of our courage and the cutting asunder of our difficulties. The fact that we have already known these pleasures to some degree in our past marriages (although they may well have been nonexistent at the time of separation) is a major incentive to strive for their attainment *in new forms in new relationships*. At the same time, however, in the emotions of divorced people, memories of past intimacy coexist with the remembered hurt of what followed from that intimacy: an abandonment emotionally equivalent to death, strengthened by echoes of parental rejection (emotionally compelling even if actually untrue) summoned up from childhood. Until we can break the conviction in our emotions that intimacy will *always* produce rejection, loss, and abandonment, relationships with the opposite sex will either be short-lived or distortive of the total personality of one or both people involved.

The more committed you become to the creative element in the divorce process, the greater the chances for breaking the intimacy-abandonment equation. First, you are becoming stronger as a separate person and therefore are freer from the poisonous need to use another person's love to validate your existence and make you feel whole. Second, you are learning to recognize the "new" in new relationships. This is what the postdivorce period of experimentation, your "second adolescence," is all about. This is when you try out new ways of coming together with members of the opposite sex in a variety of relationships—some casual, others more serious. It is a no-strings-attached time in your life when you don't drown these friendships with the requirement that they fit into a preordained pattern. It is a time of trying on new relationships with differing degrees of commitment to see how they fit your emerging single-person needs and personality, to find out what kinds of people you like and dislike, what activities and life-styles you enjoy, who you please and displease, and why. The decision to commit yourself to any great degree of intimacy will arise from the relationships themselves; the dynamics of being together will determine how you proceed.

A major impediment to sustained personal growth during this period is a hasty remarriage. Every divorce lawyer I know counsels clients not to rush into another marriage right away. Their advice is pretty well summed up in the words of one attorney to a client whose divorce had just become final: "Don't get married again for at least two years, or I'll guarantee you'll be back in my office in short order going through another break-up." Men and women who do rush into another marriage are usually those who have gotten stuck at some point in the mourning process. They still think of themselves as half-persons. They cry out, "I need someone to belong to," when they should be exploring the question, "Who do I belong *with?*"

Just as destructive, though not so prevalent, is the decision to swear off marriage completely, taken by people whose fear of future pain is so intense that they vow never again to expose themselves to the risks of closeness. "If God wanted people to get married," they say, "He would have made us Siamese twins." They, too, are just as trapped in past memories as the people who rush into a new marriage. True, they may never be hurt again, but the price they pay is denial of the life-enhancing joys of an open and intimate relationship with another person.

REMARRIAGE: WORKING
TOWARD INTIMACY

"To fear love," Bertrand Russell said, "is to fear life, and those who fear life are already three parts dead." Although few people would claim that they actually "fear" love, there are many who fear the honesty and openness from which mature love grows. They fear others won't value them if they know what they are "really" like. The best-foot-forward postures they strike to win approval from others prevent them from ever making contact with the very love and acceptance they claim they are looking for.

Yet three out of four divorced persons eventually remarry. What is it we are all looking for in a close and long-lasting relationship with a man or woman? Each of us will have a different specific answer, but I think common to them all is the desire for *intimacy:* a relationship with another person in which the risks of being open are taken daily with a constant certainty that they are outweighed by the rewards of increased directness, growing closeness and mutual trust. That trust arises from a deeply felt knowledge that each partner accepts the total personality of the other for what it is, rather than what it "should" be, and that disagreements can be resolved without either person having to give up who he or she is. Paradoxically, true intimacy is possible only when both partners are secure enough in their own autonomy that they know they can survive emotionally on their own. Only then will they be able to accept the possibility of aloneness that may result from occasional estrangements that are an inevitable part of any close relationship. Without a secure sense of self, aloneness feels tantamount to abandonment and death; with inner security, it is a temporary condition one can tolerate.

Any two people, even the most aware and articulate, are nevertheless two separate people, each of whom comes to a relationship with a particular personality and emotional history that dictate needs and expectations. If each is to maintain his own integrity, he and she must constantly test out and adjust the relationship in response to his or her own feelings, needs and limits and those of the other person. Not even the most sophisticated discussions of these differences can replace the need to work them through in the daily routine of living together—using means appropriate to the present relationship and not habits and perceptions based on memories of past marriages.

Achieving an intimate relationship far more gratifying than that which existed in your past marriage may require you to recognize, work through, and discard some old habits and patterns which developed in your previous marriage. Both you and your new partner must learn that the old ways are not the only ways love can be expressed.

You can only learn new patterns by open and direct communication of feelings and the willingness to work through disturbances as they arise. Granted, by being who we are, by expressing our feelings and setting our limits, we are vulnerable to rejection, anger, resentment, and hostility. But if the relationship is a loving one in which we do not put each other down as persons because of such disagreements, we can accept them as indications of the need to adjust the relationship—and not as attacks on our personal worth. The more we proceed according to the former assumption, the greater the trust we build into the relationship, the kind of trust we need to withstand the normal abrasions of everyday life together with another person.

THE STORY OF A
SECOND MARRIAGE

For the divorced man or woman, moving toward new intimacy means stilling that little voice that says, "Watch it. Remember what happened when you got close to someone in the past." As I was to learn myself, recognizing the pull of the past and demagnetizing it are two different things. The marriage of Rollin and Maria exemplifies the heightened gratifications possible in a second marriage despite the pain and risk they have gone through in order to let go of old habits and establish patterns appropriate to their new relationship. Both had been divorced for about three years before their marriage; in each case the first marriages had been long: thirty-one years for Rollin, and seventeen for Maria.

"We knew each other for over a year before we got married," Maria said, "and we each realized that the other had gone through a lot in our first marriages. But I don't think we realized at first how difficult it would be to disentangle ourselves from our old attitudes. Six months ago, I would have said we were on the brink of splitting up. Fortunately, we've got so much going for us that we've been able to work things out. There are still some problems with my three kids, but the worst is over."

Maria, 35, and Rollin, 51, met at a time when they were both a lot alike, but they had reached this point only after having grown out of widely divergent backgrounds. "I married my first husband to get away from my family when I was only seventeen," Maria admits. "My mother was an alcoholic and was often very violent and irrational. She controlled every aspect of my behavior. Sometimes I had to ask permission to go to the bathroom. I had to share a bedroom with three sisters. My first husband was very good-looking, but his strongest appeal was that he would take me away.

"I learned a great deal in that marriage," Maria says. "For the first time in my life I was in a decent home. We did things the 'right way,' like other families, and I was happy at first. But my ex-husband was a weak man, and he drank a lot. We had three children—two girls and then a boy—and I kind of grew up living in that family. The only trouble was, he didn't. By the end of the marriage he was still the little boy needing Mama to take care of him. His idea of life was sitting in front of the TV. He never wanted to go out or make friends on his own or take any responsibility for the kids. In fact, he seemed like one of the kids himself."

Rollin, sixteen years Maria's senior, grew up in a totally different environment. An only child, he spent many early years being shunted around foster homes, rarely living with his mother for more than six months at a time. He had married his first wife more or less out of compassion. They had known each other for about two years, but because of Rollin's military service much of that time was spent corresponding. "I visited her during a Christmas leave," Rollin remembers. "People just seemed to keep throwing us at each other. Anyway, one evening after she and her mother had had an argument and her mother had knocked her to the floor, I proposed. I guess I must have felt sorry for her. The minute I said it I wished I hadn't, but she accepted so fast I never had the courage to tell her how I really felt. That was the beginning of thirty-one years of nonsharing and noncommunication. My ex-wife said it was because of my frequent business trips, but that wasn't the whole story. She would just never let me get close to her. I remember even trying to help her with the dishes after dinner, much as I hated housework, just to be with her, but she would never let me. It's hard to believe, but in the last two years of that marriage I actually lived in the basement; we had what amounted to separate residences. No sex, no talk, no nothing. We were already divorced, but it took me two years to face the fact."

I asked Maria and Rollin what had attracted them to each other. "I had been going out with several men," Maria recalls, "most of them around my age, but they seemed so immature and unsure of themselves. When I met Rollin I thought he was a born leader, a really stable man with no hang-ups. I found him compassionate, sensitive, intelligent, and with a fantastic sense of humor. He seemed to know about everything—he's traveled a lot, plays the piano, has had a lot of experience in the world, and is a gourmet cook besides. I also appreciated his interest in my Latin American background, which is becoming more and more important to me. My first husband was always a little disappointed that I wasn't a 'real' American."

Rollin admits he was initially attracted to Maria by her physical appearance. "She was always so neat and clean, I thought she must be a very well-organized person. I also found her very attractive sexually. As we got to know each other I was tremendously impressed with how well she had overcome a really miserable childhood. I think that was an important bond at first, we had both been so unhappy as children.

"The biggest thrill for me, though, was talking with a woman who was so articulate about her feelings, and so interested in mine. After the party when we first met, we spent two hours just sitting in my car, talking. I found myself telling her things I had never said to anyone. At one point she leaned over and kissed me on the cheek. We hadn't touched before then. It aroused me something fierce, just a little kiss of understanding. I had never experienced that combination of sexual arousal and tenderness before.

"We started going out regularly after that, although I was put off at first by the difference in our ages. I also had this terrible feeling that I was repeating the past. I mean, was I really in love with her, or was it the same kind of compassion that made me propose to my first wife?"

Both Rollin and Maria agree that they went into this marriage with a far clearer idea of what their mate was really like than they did the first time around. Neither feels fooled at having bought a knight-in-shining-armor package, and yet they are finding the day-to-day life together of two mature people not without problems. "Luckily, we've got enough that's really good—the sex, our interest in people, our general personalities, you could say—so that we're weathering the little storms. One reason is that we're both open about what we feel. Neither of us can blame the other the way we did with our first spouses. Nor do we always assume we know what the other person is thinking. The thing about marrying someone you realize has lived a lot before he met you is that you feel this need to check things out fairly regularly. I think that's good."

They both pinpoint the issue of "togetherness" as the major problem so far in their relationship. "I realized Rollin had felt deprived of love as a child and as a husband," Maria says, "but I was unaware that my response to his need for attention would be so strong. I've had to struggle very hard for my identity and independence, and now that I feel I've got it, I don't want to give it up. Quiet time by myself—when I can read, or play the piano, or just sit—is very important to me. It was hard enough juggling three kids and teaching art and ceramics twenty-five hours a week after my divorce. When we got married, Rollin wanted some time alone with me. Of course I want to be with him, too, but I also need time for myself and the children and my other interests.

"We had talked about this before we got married, and Rollin was very sympathetic to my need for independence, but when it got down to specifics there were problems. He'd sit right next to me on the piano seat, or interrupt a television program the kids and I were watching, and once or twice he even came to my classes. He said he just wanted to be with me, wasn't that the reason we got married? At first he used to ask me to have lunch with him in his office. Well, sometimes I only had a half-hour between classes and it was really hard to make time for him. Lunch was the only time I had to prepare material for the afternoon sessions. He just never let me *be*. During the first six months I found myself giving up friends, my music, my quiet times by myself. The only things left were my work and the kids. And my own sense of myself. I was getting really resentful. Once I shouted at him, 'You're swallowing me, just like the children! Do I have to spend every waking minute with you to prove I love you?' "

"She scared me when she said that," Rollin recalls. "You know, I never asked her to give up those things, but I can see now I must have been applying some not-so-subtle pressure. Strangely enough, the first inkling I had came from a remark my ex-wife made. We were meeting to discuss a leftover question of property settlement and at one point, she exploded. She said life with me had been thirty-one years of hell for her, that I was still just a little boy tugging on her apron strings. It sounded so much like what Maria had said about my swallowing her up that I began to wonder if I was being as open and direct as I had thought."

Rollin's question, and Maria's growing resentment, prompted them to go to a family counselor, in the conviction that theirs was a marriage worth saving. What they learned was that, despite their honest expression of feelings in all other areas, the memories of the past were interfering with their ability to work through this problem. Maria, although she recognized the basic difference between Rollin and her first husband, was reacting to his insistence on time together with her in the context of her ex-husband's demands. He had always required her to cater to his needs. She could never express her need for breathing room to her ex-husband. She thought it wasn't "nice," that wives weren't supposed to feel this way. She was repeating the pattern with Rollin: rather than asserting herself at the time she felt imposed upon, she would hoard her resentments until they spilled out three days later in an angry outburst. This produced in her a feeling of guilt for having gotten angry, and further confused her understanding of the difference between anger and assertion. An additional circumstance from Maria's past which exacerbated her reaction to Rollin's intrusions was the memory of her mother's absolute dominance over Maria's life, against which Maria felt powerless to express herself. The effect on Rollin of Maria's internal stresses was a growing hostility toward Maria and an increasing tendency to hear in her angry outbursts echoes of his former wife's rejection of him.

Once they understood what was happening, they were able to concentrate on the differences between their present and past marriages, and to hear behind the familiar demands for attention (and autonomy) the different motivations, and the love which each held for the other. "It's easy to sit here and talk about it now," Rollin says, "but it's damned hard to break patterns that you have lived with all your life. We thought we were being open with each other, but this is one area we weren't so open about. Maria feels better now about setting her limits right when she feels I'm intruding (instead of collecting resentments and letting me have it days later) and I do my best to give her the space she wants. Since we really do love and trust each other, we are trying to accept the reasons behind each other's needs. I still sneak out to the kitchen for cookies and milk when I feel cut off, and she says there are times when she feels pulled in all directions at once, but at least we don't resent the other any more."

The more they express their real feelings, the better they feel their relationship is becoming. "Each time we're really honest with each other and the marriage doesn't fly apart, we grow closer," Rollin says. "Another thing that's helped is her kids. The closer we become the less we all cling to Maria as a point of contact. At first we saw each other as competitors of her time, but we're slowly becoming friends. Alex, the eight-year-old, is the closest to me now. When Maria and I first got married he used to growl at me, actually growl. We couldn't figure out what was going on, until Maria found out he had been reading a book about tigers and thought that by growling at me he could scare me off. Now he calls me Daddy. When his older sisters complain that I'm 'hogging up' their mother, he always comes to my defense. As Alex puts it, 'Rollin married us.' His sisters are taking longer to get used to me. Linda, the fourteen-year-old, once said she didn't understand why her mother married such an old man, old men have had more time to develop more hang-ups. She and her sister were really affected by the divorce and are angry at men in general. Their father hasn't paid a dime to support them and they resent that bitterly—but they're coming to accept me more and more."

"Whatever our problems—and we've had some—they're only problems because we care so much for each other that we won't hide what we feel. We both know from our past marriages what happens when you get started on that road. We're willing to admit the disturbances we've got because we've got the kind of love and tenderness and acceptance we've never had before, and we won't give those up without a damned hard fight."

HERE WE
GO AGAIN?

As Rollin and Maria have discovered, patterns of past relationships can cloud the present for even the most perceptive man or woman, especially when the past crops up in new forms. Joel, 43, came to one of my seminars when his second marriage had broken up after less than two years, and he was at a loss to know why. "My first marriage lasted eighteen years. I came from the midwest, and my first wife came from Vermont. She was what some people might think of as the typical New England woman: hard-working, taciturn, not very demonstrative or emotional. Somehow she always managed to rig things so that I felt guilty. Nothing I ever did was good enough for her, although she never came out and said so. Whenever I did something by myself, like playing golf on Saturday morning, I got the definite impression from her that I was an inconsiderate slob. I lived with the old martyr bit, the 'if you don't know what's wrong I can't tell you' routine.

"After we got divorced, I was bound and determined I wouldn't make the same mistake again. I actually made a list of all the qualities I wanted in a woman: warmth, affection, spontaneity, the ability to enjoy a good laugh. When I met Inez, I thought I had it all. She couldn't have been more different from my first wife—born in Venezuela, very emotional and outgoing, not so house-proud, and extremely attractive sexually. Physically, there was no resemblance: she was short and dark and round, while my first wife was tall, fair, and angular. Inez and I got married five months after my divorce became final, and eighteen months later we split up. I just couldn't stand her tears and tantrums. The slightest thing would send her off the deep end. I was constantly in the position of having to apologize for something I knew nothing about. I felt like I should greet her every day with 'Good morning, and I'm sorry.' "

Joel's problem was that, in zeroing in on the external differences between his first and second wives, he had ignored something within himself to which both his wives, each in her own way, had responded: his equation of love with domination and control. He associated control with love because that was the combination his mother evidenced in the course of bringing him up. His first wife had managed through silent suffering, his second by means of emotional outbursts, but the effect on Joel was the same. Although his need to be dominated in order to feel loved was clearly in conflict with other parts of his personality (thus his two divorces), the signals he was sending out were strong enough to attract at least two controlling women. The solution to his problem lay not in making lists of those qualities he wanted in a wife, but in facing squarely the conflicts within himself which guaranteed his involvement with the kind of woman from whom he would eventually turn away.

The phenomenon of the divorced man or woman unconsciously marrying a carbon copy (either physically or emotionally) of his former mate is well known. Quite often it takes an offhand comment by a friend for these people to recognize how closely they have repeated the past. Conversely, sometimes we may see the past in new relationships when it really isn't there. Similar actions of two different people do not necessarily spring from the same motivation, nor carry the same connotation. However, making this distinction at the emotional level is not always easy, as Lucille, 35, found out with her second mother-in-law. "She is a very helpful woman," Lucille said. "I know she is delighted that John and I got married. She's said many times how much happier her son seems now than he did during his first marriage. I really do like her a lot, but every time she offers some well-meaning assistance, my mind flashes back to my first mother-in-law. That woman and I never got along. She was convinced I was a bad mother and a sloppy house-keeper. She used to stop by with baskets of hot food. Otherwise, as she told me, she would worry herself sick over whether John was getting enough to eat. Well, last week my new mother-in-law came over with a strawberry pie she had baked. I got furious and accused her of thinking I didn't know how to cook. Later I realized the wrong connection I had unconsciously made between her and my first mother-in-law, and apologized. She said she's always enjoyed baking pies for her friends with strawberries from her own garden. She was being generous and here I had thought she was being meddlesome and critical."

Tom and Peggy, both previously wed, experienced another kind of intrusion from the past early in their marriage. Tom, a college teacher, noticed after about four months that following every dinner party they hosted, Peggy would pick a fight over some trivial event and end the evening by running into the bedroom, slamming the door, and crying. After four or five such outbursts, Tom became annoyed, but he also began to sense a pattern: during each dinner Peggy would be edgy and self-conscious. At some point during the party she would draw Tom aside and tell him he wasn't talking enough to the guests. Tom would reply that he had spent that afternoon lecturing and was now enjoying the rare opportunity to listen and respond to others without having to hold forth as the voice of authority. Somehow, though, Peggy—who was in all other circumstances extremely understanding of the pressures of Tom's work—never found this explanation satisfactory.

The truth emerged one evening after a particularly tempestuous postparty fight. It turned out that Peggy had bitterly resented the fact that her first husband refused to enter into his role as host. On the one hand she felt he demanded that the food, the house, the flowers—everything she was in charge of—had to be perfect, but to her he would never lift a finger to circulate among the guests or draw them out. Because she was afraid of criticizing her ex-husband directly, she would vent her feelings indirectly by picking a fight over some other matter and then overreacting in tears and slammed doors. It was her way of punishing him for being a silent host. Although in every other way she felt Tom was very different from her first husband, the slightest tendency on his part toward similar behavior in a similar situation (regardless of the difference in motivation) catapulted her back into an emotional response from the past. Peggy still gets twinges of anger when she feels Tom is too quiet at a party, but these twinges are no longer indirectly expressed through seemingly unrelated arguments, tears, and slammed doors. And as time passes, Tom's manifest difference from her first husband (and the frequent checking-out of each other's feelings) are helping to erase past memories.

The period of experimentation following a divorce is tailor-made for discovering—and breaking—patterns from the past. Janet, 33, had been going out with Mark for a month. They seemed to get along very well, except that Janet became increasingly frustrated by her inability to express her own feelings with him. Matters built to a head one evening when Mark's unilateral decision that they should eat in a Mexican restaurant opened the floodgates and all Janet's pent-up hostility poured out. The next day a friend pointed out to Janet that either she had a pathological dislike of Mexican food or there was some serious problem in her relationship with Mark. Upon reflection, Janet realized that her inability to express disagreement with her ex-husband (on anything from where they should spend vacations to what they should watch on television) had been a prime cause of their divorce, and thereupon she decided to be more assertive with Mark. They continued to see each other for the next few weeks, but eventually broke apart—he to find a woman who would let him make all the decisions, she to find a man who was not threatened by an assertive woman. "I missed him for a while," Janet said later, "but more the way you would miss a favorite pair of gloves. Ye Gods, imagine getting myself back into that scene! I'm sure I must scare off some men, but I'm learning that I couldn't be happy with that type in the long run. And anyway, I seem to be attracting a more confident breed these days. It's still an effort to be honest, but it's getting easier—and it's much more satisfying than going through life with a vapid smile on your face."

Bruce, 29, discovered an important pattern from his past marriage when he was sharing an apartment with another man. At a meeting of his group, Bill said he was hoping to get married again soon, because his roommate was driving him crazy. "We share the rent, but Fred runs the show," he complained. "Even on double dates, he decides where we're going, and once we get there he does all the talking. It's really frustrating." Several members of the group smiled at the obvious "odd couple" overtones of Bruce's tale, but he insisted that during his marriage he had worn the pants in the family. Upon further thought, he identified the similarity between his relationship with his ex-wife and his present roommate: in both instances he felt there was no way he could say what was bothering him without tearing up the relationship. Because his friendship with his roommate was not nearly so important as his relationship with his wife had been, Bruce felt he could risk asserting his feelings with Fred. As he saw each act of assertion straighten things out rather than tear things up, he was moved to proceed further, until he reported that they were managing to live together with minimum friction. "He still thinks he's king of the mountain," said Bruce, "but I tell him where I stand and he accepts it with pretty good grace. And I'm putting my newfound skill to good use with women. They tell me they like a man who speaks his mind."

A common pattern of past marriages which frequently is tossed by the wayside before remarriage is what I call the Frog-Prince Fantasy, in honor of Alice, 34, a woman in one of my seminars. Alice said, "After my divorce, I went out with two or three men who were the despair of all my friends. They kept asking me what I saw in such jerks. I thought I had some special gift for bringing out hidden depths in people. It took me six months to realize that this was just what I had tried to do with my ex-husband. I thought I could turn him from a frog into a prince. Well, I kissed and kissed and kissed but after thirteen years he was still a frog. You've got to accept a person for what he is, as the saying goes, and not waste time trying to change them into something that they can't or don't want to be."

The trap of reading one's own expectations into another person is easier to fall into if the other person does not present a clear and accurate picture of who he is. One of the reasons many women are attracted to the strong, silent type is just this temptation they offer to build castles in the air. Leonard, 47, fit the bill perfectly. His first marriage ended when his wife became disgusted with his moodiness, lack of sociability, and stoic responses. Now he was going with a woman who he said admired him for his assurance, manliness, quiet charm, and insight. "Hell, it's nice to know she thinks I'm that great," he said, "but I don't really see that I'm all that wonderful. Mostly I just agree with what she says." To her, he is a blank sheet of paper for her to fill in with her own fantasies.

DEGREES OF COMMITMENT

Many divorced people who are exploring the boundaries of their own personalities find support in changing social mores. Whatever the tag line—"becoming your own person," "the human potential movement," "lifelong learning"—there is a slowly growing groundswell of approval for the person with the courage to go where his needs and abilities take him. Laura, 35, put it this way: "People are always accusing the women's movement of breaking up marriages. I don't think that's true, except that the movment has made some people who got married mainly because of social pressure do some hard thinking about the kinds of marriages they have. Take me. There I was, four years out of college. All my friends were getting married, and my parents kept twisting my arm in subtle little ways. It just seemed to be 'time to get married.' You know, like there's a time for college, and a time to have a dinky job, and then it's time to get married. So I did, but that's not much of a reason. I had to keep my 'dinky little job' as secretary after we got married, and after a couple of years they made me an associate editor and I started enjoying the responsibility. My husband blames our divorce on the fact that my job made me too independent. It wasn't the money; he still made a lot more than I did. What bothered him so much was the fact that I really liked my job, while he was just plugging along in a boring rut. We weren't even friends when we broke up, so why should we have stayed in a marriage and killed each other off? My next marriage, if and when, will have to make room for me, Laura, and part of me is my job. You know, if I had said this ten years ago people would really have put me down. Now it's the ones who just stew in their own juice who may be out of step."

As expectations for marriage center more on the wish for a deep and open emotional commitment and less on parenthood, status, and economic security, there is a growing trend among all men and women—and especially those who have been divorced—to test out their commitment in stages. They have enjoyed the "falling in love with love" experience, but they no longer believe that Cupid's arrow is any guarantee of foreverness. They have learned the truth of what Sir Walter Scott wrote almost two hundred years ago: "What we love in the early days is generally rather a fanciful creation of our own than a reality. We build statues of snow and weep when they melt." In the absence of external supports that once stabilized matrimony, people are approaching marriage with a caution that matches their high expectations for a union of openness, autonomy, and authentic intimacy. They want time to learn about themselves and their partners in the context of living together, rather than trusting to impressions gained during courtship. As one divorced woman said, "I learned my lesson the first time. It didn't take me long to realize that what I knew about my husband when we were going together I could put on the head of a pin. All I saw was the tip of the iceberg. That's all I really wanted to see, I was so anxious to get married."

Freed from what a West Coast columnist has called the poison of need, more people are trying out living-together arrangements which do not require promises of a commitment beyond what they are prepared to give. I applaud the sentiments of the divorced men and women in second marriages who are prepared to work twice as hard to make their second marriages a success. However, when I detect deep-seated fears of "failing again," I sometimes think that Dennis, 35 and an avowed antiestablishment college teacher, may also be on the right track: "I know that I need the satisfaction of an intimate and lasting relationship with a woman, but I really wonder if we can expect any relationship like that to last forever? Things and people are changing so fast today that maybe ten years is the most we can hope for. When I got married the first time it was going to be a lifetime thing. Well, it wasn't and I survived. I've been living with a woman now for about three years. She's just finished her doctoral dissertation in history and is beginning to look for a teaching job. Faculty openings are scarce these days, and she may well have to move to another state in order to find work. We've talked a lot about what this will mean to our relationship, and right now we don't know what we'll do if we're faced with that decision. Maybe one or both of us will commute. Maybe we'll break up; it would be rough but we could both take it. We know we both need our work to make us happy. We need each other, too. There's a lot of love between us. We don't know what will happen, but we do know we will have to test the strengths of our commitments to our work and to each other. We'll just have to wait and see what happens."

There are many kinds of living-together arrangements (known in some circles as LTA's). Perhaps most common are the courtship unions of young people who move in together with an understanding that perhaps they will eventually marry. There are LTAs in which both partners seem to be flaunting their life-style as a sign of social liberation; these are often brief. Then there are the frankly manipulative relationships in which a woman (or a man) is kept in exchange for sexual favors, or to perform as a socially acceptable consort at public appearances. Whatever the motivations, LTAs are the subject of a great deal of media attention these days: where to live (your place? my place? a new place?); what to tell the landlord and the neighbors; how to handle financial affairs, extracurricular sex, dishwashing duties, children.

A growing portion of living-together arrangements are made up of previously married men and women, many of them in the over-thirty age bracket, who are willing to struggle with their still-powerful feelings of guilt in order to test out the quality of a new relationship. What is the impact on them of this style of living? Is it a valuable learning experience, or in the long run does it diminish their sense of self-esteem? I put the question recently to Liza, a thirty-one-year-old divorced woman with no children who had just broken up an LTA of two years' standing. "On balance, I'd say it was a learning experience," she said. "I learned I could be a good partner. I grew a lot as a person, and I'd do it again. This time, though, I'd try to be more honest with myself. When I moved in with Peter I *said* it was only temporary, but deep in my mind must have been the hope that it would be permanent. And Peter, for all his verbal support of women's liberation, expected dinner to be on the table when he got home and raised hell if it wasn't. During the last six months it turned into a bad marriage even without the piece of paper: I gained fifteen pounds and felt I was walking on eggs all the time trying to please him. We never saw any of my friends because I thought he wouldn't approve of them. It broke up when I joined a women's consciousness-raising group. That's when he got uptight, and we split. I got my knuckles rapped for expressing my own needs, just like when I was married. But this time I went with what I knew I had to do, and it was the right decision."

Sharon, 35, has been living with Stanley for a year and a half. She ascribes a great deal of the success of their relationship to the fact that both she and Stanley had been divorced before. "Each of us had been the one to initiate the divorce," she said. "I think because of that we pay more attention to our relationship. We both respect the fact that we can survive without the other, but because we enjoy being together we don't take each other for granted."

Sharon said she would never have predicted she would find herself in a living-together arrangement. "When I divorced my first husband I was in no condition to even think about another man. That was a really bad marriage. I was twenty when we married, and all I really knew about my ex-husband was that he was good-looking and was going to be a doctor. What I didn't know was that he was self-centered, punitive, and more interested in his real estate investments than in our marriage. Eleven years later we had progressed beyond the graduate student life-style in every way but in Jason's mind. He still thought I was Dumb Dora, and he was the carefree kid. He never would make plans more than a day in advance, or ask me what I thought about anything. Every weekend he would be gone—'looking into real estate,' he said, but it was just an excuse to go camping by himself. He sank all our money in land. In the meantime, I had gotten a job in the public information office of the art museum, and was beginning to get the idea that I wasn't quite as dependent on him as he always insisted. In fact, I was the one who broke up the marriage, and he was the one who fell apart. I practically had to have him evicted, and he's still got me tangled up in legal battles."

In the months following her separation Sharon went out with a number of men, but she felt so gun-shy that she kept her dating very casual. "I'd go out with some guy I found attractive and interesting—even sleep with him—but whenever things got serious I backed off. I kept things on a physical level—partly, I think, so I wouldn't let myself get sucked into idolizing some man again. This went on for about a year, and I met a lot of different men. It wasn't just sex. I had some men friends who would come over in the evening with a pizza or something and we'd kill a bottle of wine and just talk. But after a while the whole scene began to bore me. I think when I met Stan I was ready for something more.

"We met at a party and hit it off immediately. He was funny, bright, attentive, and sexy—no Burt Reynolds, but he had a personality that really turned me on. We started going out, and the more I got to know him the more I liked him. He's eight years older than I am, but we're very compatible. We both liked things in each other that our former mates had criticized: I liked his casual, long hairstyle, and he liked my spontaneous qualities and my interest in other people."

Sharon says they slowly drifted together without any long-range planning, although as she looks back on it now, living together seemed inevitable. "We both continued to go out with other people, but we started seeing each other more and more until we were together every evening. I found myself laughing and smiling much more than ever before. Of course by this time we were sleeping together, and the sex was more than just physical, it was tender, and more satisfying than in all my married years. We talked about what we liked, as against my husband who was very closemouthed on the subject of sex, and we were spontaneous. We still are. Sometimes in the morning, in the afternoon, once in the dining room. I like that kind of unexpected fun. And it's good—better than with other men after my divorce and certainly better than with Jason. Until my divorce I never knew what prolonged intercourse was. With Jason it was always fast—here-it-comes, there-it-goes."

Sharon feels their relationship has progressed on a continuum toward greater and greater intimacy. "At first we were both feeling so burned by our last marriages we didn't want to make any kind of commitment that sounded permanent," she admits. "We both were afraid it would spoil things. Deciding to actually live together was a big step, because we both felt we should find a new place, neither his nor mine. Moving in together was itself a big commitment that our relationship means a lot to us both. It was as much as we felt we could make at that time. Our apartment is a symbol of our new start together. That was a very risky time for us both, and I think for a while we felt somewhat inhibited by the permanence of it all, but we were both reluctant to admit it. I even had a flare-up of my old asthma attack, which I only get when I'm really uptight about something. Fortunately, though, we were building up a foundation of trust that was strong enough by then to let us express our reservations and work through them."

At this stage of their relationship Sharon says they are beginning to think they might get married. "It's only been recently that we've actually been able to talk about it without getting skittish. I think we'll probably get married soon: we both look at marriage as the only way to make a statement about our commitment to each other. I think if we had gotten married any earlier we'd still be preoccupied with out past fears."

I asked Sharon if she had any advice for others who might be contemplating living together, and she brought up an issue many divorced men and women have raised in my seminars: children. "Don't get the idea this has all been a bed of roses," she said. "Now I look back on it and it all seems right, but at the time there were daily uncertainties. The biggest problem we had to face was Stan's three children—two teen-age girls and a boy ten years old. His older daughter and I didn't get along at all at first. We were both locked in some kind of competitive thing. I resented any time he spent with his kids, and they hated me. His ex-wife didn't make it any easier. She was dating a lawyer and she actually had him sit down with the kids and read them the penal code about adultery. She had them convinced I was the homewrecker, even though Stan and I didn't meet until after his divorce.

"In the last six months they've begun to be friendlier. The girls, especially, see that I'm not trying to stand between them and their father, or take their money from him as his ex-wife thinks. He always has the last word on discipline. To tell you the truth, though, his kids are one of the reasons for our decision to get married soon. Stan was really cut up by his ex-wife's attitude toward us, only because of what she told the kids about us. She won't let him call them; they have to phone him, and she insists they reverse the charges when they call. More than once he's actually wept over the thought that she will turn them from him completely. I think once we're married we'll both feel better about insisting on certain kinds of behavior from them. And I think they will respond to me better once I have some status beyond being 'Daddy's girl friend.' Stan told me once his little boy asked why he should be polite to me, because he thought I wasn't going to be around very long. It seems to me that part of getting married will be to show them I'm here to stay. And I'll feel better about being with them."

The feelings of guilt which underly much of Sharon's feelings about Stan's children cannot be denied, especially in mature men and women who have been raised according to older standards concerning the sanctity of marriage. One fifty-two-year-old man whose eighteen-month LTA ended in marriage put it this way: "We just felt less tight inside after we got married. I guess the guilt trip was too much for us; maybe kids today can hack it, but we had to face the fact that we really didn't feel as comfortable as we wanted to. Besides, neither of us is very far-out when it comes to our likes and dislikes, and we find now that we're married we have a more varied social life. I'm sure some people disapproved of how we were living before, but more important I think was that we presented a threat to them, the possibility that we were so damned independent one of us might latch onto one of them. Anyway, we feel much more secure now. I'm enough of a child of my parents to like the security of being married. We tried it the other way and it was all right, but we just reached a point where we felt we had to be married to grow further."

Each relationship—be it marriage, a living-together arrangement, or casual dating—proceeds according to its own dynamics. Each of the examples in this chapter is unique in many respects, but there is a steady progression in most of them toward the kind of closeness and intimacy between two separate individuals that most divorced men and women are looking for. Each step in this direction is both an affirmation of the desire for intimacy and a test of whether that intimacy will enhance or diminish the autonomy of each partner. For the divorced man or woman it is a journey with perils: does this particular disagreement arise over real differences between us, or am I treating my partner and our relationship as if I were still in my past marriage? Like Rollin and many, many others, forging an intimate relationship often requires the unlearning of past habits of loving, and the relearning of more appropriate ways of perceiving and acting.

The relationship between intimacy and growth is perhaps best expressed in these words of two family therapists, "For adults, creative growth must involve areas of shared intimacies and mutual goals. . . . Each may be dependent on the other in many ways but not for survival. Each is responsible for his own growth. His survival must be dependent on his ability to achieve that growth through open and direct expression of his desires and limitations. The marital partners must be able to accept such expression from each other as an indication of their differentness. This involves perceiving differentness at its best as potentially enhancing to the relationship, and at its worst as somewhat limiting. If perceived as an attack or intent to undermine, the relationship cannot grow. A 'working' marital relationship in reality, then, is not a blending or meshing of two individuals into a whole person. It is the accomplishment of two individuals who remain intact in their individuality so that their individual growth evolves concurrently. Ideally, the growth of each is then enhanced by the growth of the other. . . ."*

* "Survival Patterns in Family Conjoint Therapy—Myth and Reality," by S. Gerke and M. Kirschenbaum. Family Service Agency of Marin County, California.

TO SAY GOOD-BYE
IS TO SAY HELLO

> In all beginnings dwells a magic force
> For guarding us and helping us to live ...

These words by Herman Hesse, novelist and poet, speak directly to the millions of divorced men and women embarking on the journey toward new commitments. Hesse himself experienced the trauma of divorce twice in his lifetime. By his third marriage, however, he had rid himself of his lingering need to seek out a substitute mother, a childish need which had tainted his first two marriages. He was able, then, at the age of fifty-four, to form a mature relationship free of unrealistic expectations. This marriage lasted thirty-one years and encompassed the period of his most profound writing.

"Be ready bravely and without remorse," Hesse wrote, "to find new light that old ties cannot give." It is my belief that the creative divorce process can foster the self-awareness and security necessary for such a quest. My goal has been to write the kind of book I wish had been in existence when I went through my own divorce crisis: a book which avoids glib responses to complicated problems that do not yield to easy answers; a book with a perspective which could explain to me the reasons behind the apparently unrelated changes in my life and could show me how to regain control; and finally a book which would offer realistic hopes and suggest goals I could strive for and eventually achieve.

I am gratified that so many of the men and women in my seminars have sought to renew their lives through the creative divorce process at a time when they had given up almost all hope that the future held any pleasures for them. Their decision to risk the new was difficult, for old habits and ways of looking at the world are hard to break, but they have found their personal growth as rewarding as the degree of effort they were able to put into it.

Fortunately, no one need follow this path unaided. For the men and women with a real desire to grow who are also willing to translate this desire into action, today's world offers a great deal of help, from popular periodicals to professional assistance—including within this span adult education and career counseling programs, books, special-purpose organizations, and the insights of friends and family. While none of these provide motivation to grow—this only you can supply—they can offer insights, emotional support, and practical assistance. If you have the motivation to improve the quality of your life, you will act on whatever eye-opening suggestions you find in these resources for self-renewal. If you don't act, either your motivation is not as great as you think, or your problems may be such that you need some further professional assistance. For those divorced people trapped in the mourning process who continue to live in the past and cannot see the opportunities in the present, professional assistance is entirely warranted. Trained men and women—whether they call themselves psychiatrists, psychologists, psychotherapists, psychoanalysts, counselors, therapists, or psychiatric social workers—can help people discover and deal with problems so that they can resume effective management of their lives.

It is my hope that each separated or divorced person will see in this book a path toward a new beginning. Each of you must apply its contents to your own experience, and on that basis draw your own conclusions as to where your future lies. I see the opportunity before every divorced man or woman to use the crisis of divorce to begin a new life, a life that recognizes the best of the past, accepts the challenges of the present, and is open to the newness of each new day.